The Criminal Housewife
by
Jean Samuel McConnell

The Criminal Housewife
by
Jean Samuel McConnell

(c) 2001 by Jean Samuel McConnell

Published by
Lone Oak Press
1412 Bush Street,
Red Wing, Minnesota 55066
info@loneoak.org
ISBN 1-883477-46-8
Library of Congress Control Number: 2001099261

Contents

The Criminal Housewife

CHAPTER 1

Zack Taylor said, "That simple minded son of a bitch. He overruled me. Several times. He was dead wrong every time."

Tom DeShales was laconic. "Matter of opinion. Maybe his honorableness was correct. You do carry on at times. Matter of fact you carry on most of the time. Need a tight rein, thinks his judgeship."

"'Course I carry on. Makes me a colorful attorney. Hell, it's all I got going for me. Had to take the bar exam three times, without color I'm dead meat."

"Three times? Thought it was four."

"Well, maybe. I might have disremembered." Zack Taylor reeled in his line and flicked it out again into the calm waters of Lake Pepin. "Are there any fish in this friggin' place? I mean live ones, that the P.C.B.'s haven't finished off."

"Well," said DeShales, "I've managed to hook three in an hour. You don't know your ass from third base about fishing. You can't bait a hook properly, you can't cast as good as a six year old. You're good at one thing, though."

"Here it comes."

"You can bitch and moan about judges."

"Well, they're all incompetent."

"Of course they're incompetent. That's how lousy lawyers get to be round head judges. It's the system. Our forefathers, in their infinite wisdom, decreed that we must have idiot judges to keep lawyers sharp trying to outwit them."

"Is that how it happened? Knew there had to be some insane reason."

The boat drifted slowly, oars shipped, motor silent, in the gentle swells. Late May sunshine dappled the water. On this inland lake, a mere swollen artery of the old Mississippi, the two friends sought surcease from the swirled spaghetti of the legal system. One half mile away, toward the Wisconsin shore, a barge of staggering length moved at its glacial pace upstream, too far removed from any ripple effect on the fishing boat.

"Four times, huh?"

"Four what?"

"Your exams. How did you finally make it?"

"What is this, a trick question? I cheated, of course."

"Pardon my ignorance."

"It wasn't all cheating. After a few times you get a feeling about what they want. The Board that is, whoever those devious people are, and, you know, you kind of slant your thinking along those lines."

"Certainly, but, being somewhat brilliant, I did that the first time, didn't need all those dry runs. Damn it." Tom's voice wailed as his line went taut, then limp. "Son of a bitch got away. Heavy pull, must of been a lunker."

"Or the guard rail off an old snowmobile. Must be a dozen down there. Metallic stuff is hard to land."

"I often wondered," said Tom DeShales, "why so many of those Arctic Cats and Polaris machines end up down there."

"Well, sun shines, ice gets thin – not an easy principle to grasp."

"Like your specialty?"

"Ho boy, my specialty. I am a certified, highly educated member of the Minnesota Bar – available for just causes."

"Like ambulance chaser. Get there soonest, before the blood is dry."

Zack Taylor chuckled. "Ah well, food on the table. Hungry kids, wife with a hollow leg, and look who's preaching: Tom DeShales, boot licker to every land developer in this end of the state."

"You wound me deeply, Zack."

"My sympathy."

"I am wounded because somebody has to hawkeye those damn plats. Make sure the sewer and water lines don't get crossed up. You ever taste water out of a sewer pipe? Tastes like shit. Hell, it is shit."

He sighed. "But it's the commercial that's tough. Strip malls. I'd prefer strip joints."

"Like Jack's?"

"Now you're talking. They've got a new one there – 46-24-36. So they say. Well, they got as much right to lie as the car dealers, I guess. Still – very impressive."

A desultory quietness descended upon the two friends. They fished in silence for a spell. Zack finally made his day with a two pounder. "I'll never eat the damn thing, but a neighbor guy likes 'em," he muttered. "Why is it that fish taste so bad but fishing is God's great gift to the working stiff?"

"Well, I love them. Walleye or Pike over T-bone anytime. And crappies are great."

"P.C.B.'s and all?"

"Aw, hell, there's something in everything. Hormones in the beef, stuff in the milk, pesticides in the lettuce and radishes – all that stuff. That marvelous machine, the body, well, maybe not your lardass body, sifts it out. We get by."

"Me, I'm always on the lookout for a good environmental case. Sock it to those blasted chemical firms. Man, that's deep pockets. Deep, clear to the ankles."

"Not me, but it's your gig, personal injury. Whiplash, all that stuff. Why not poison to the system, from the automobile, the air, the water, the food? Lawn chemicals, there's a vast uncharted field out there. And it's your specialty. Me? Just wrangle those new developments. Wrangle, wrangle with the land owners, planning and zoning board – you really have to suck up to that strange outfit. Then there's the Mayor and City Council. Is that a circus! You know, I've often thought, those guys in the Revolutionary War fought for freedom, the freedom for uninformed voters to stick us with a bunch of clowns."

"That bad? I don't have much to do with them."

"Bad? You have no idea. A couple of them are smart enough to know how dumb they are. The others haven't got a clue. Therefore, not knowing they're idiots, they think they're brilliant. Still, they can be conned, so I count my blessings."

"I thought I was the bitter one."

Tom DeShales grinned.

"Aw, I'm not bitter. I make a living. They aren't really that bad. I was laying it on a bit thick."

"In a growing city, officials have their hands full. New regs, new annexations and such."

"Of course."

"You do real good though," said Zack Taylor. "Me, I've been in a slump. Would let my secretary go if she wasn't such a stack. What I'd give for a smash-up on I-90. Fourteen cars tailgating into each other, and I get to shill for all of 'em."

"Can't you help it along, grease the highway, something like that?"

"Hey, you unethical?"

"Never."

"Me too." Zack yawned, he had never felt more relaxed and peaceful as the late spring sun warmed him. No money, prospects poor, but what the hell, things have a way of coming around. He had lived most of his life in southern Minnesota and had always practiced in the lovely, progressive city of Crestburg. Not a metropolis, more than a small town, Zack had never really desired to live elsewhere, never tempted to hang his shingle in the bustling melee of the Twin Cities.

Tom DeShales was also content. But he was a man who did things in measured segments. Now for him the fishing was over. "Hey," he said. "Lets pull in to shore. Couple of nice taverns on the Minnesota, side. I could go for a foamy brew.

"What a salesman! Sold!"

"All salesmen should have a mark like you."

The healing power of fishing had worked its magic once again. Cares vanished in the balmy air. Zack Taylor had a son he could not communicate with and DeShales' marriage was leaking like a punctured lifeboat. Personal trouble follows most folks, even in a regional super star city like Crestburg. The usual disappointments, heartaches, blasted dreams were joined at the hip with contentment and family happiness. One such family resided in a modest, small house in an older part of town where elms and maples lined the streets in shaded canopy.

At eight A.M. each day, Galen Janes went to work at the Cardinal Hardware Store. At five thirty he returned home, worked in the garden. In the cold months, he worked at his bench in the basement.

At seven, the family, what remained of the family, had their evening meal. Then T.V., a small bowl of cereal or fruit and ice cream, then to bed. This was Monday through Friday. Every other Saturday was half day at work.

"This," said Cass, his wife, "is a pace we simply can't keep up. The excitement is getting to me, we've got to slow down. Agree?"

"Um.

"Next thing you know we'll be going to Bingo Night at the Legion Hall."

"Play three cards."

"Here's another slice of cardiac arrest: Wednesday night at St. Olaf's for lutefisk and lefsa. And – and, get this, a grab or two on the pull tabs."

"You're getting my ticker racing."

"First time in quite a while."

"I don't hold with you getting too much."

Cass rolled her eyes. "Here's another thing. Most of the people we know get out of these snow banks for a spell each winter. It's not winter right now, but you know what I mean."

"Like who?"

"The Hanson's for like who. Bill and Gerry Carpenter, the Ellison's."

"Who the hell are the Ellison's?"

"You've met them. You just don't remember. She's a friend of mine. I think he sells real estate. Or maybe it's trucks."

"Sixty thousand people in this town. You've come up with six."

"There's more, believe it."

"The point?"

"Why don't we go to Florida, or Texas or Arizona for a change next winter?"

"Can't get away. Work. We take a two week vacation in August you know."

"I know. Another huge thrill, stalking the wily walleye. And I hate cleaning those suckers."

"Well, I mostly do that chore."

"Well, yes, I'll admit that." Cass fetched the coffeepot and poured the refills. "To hell with your piddly vacation, take a leave. You've been there long enough."

"Company policy. No go."

The quiet in the old kitchen was, suddenly, stifling. Cass and Galen were reenacting a familiar scene. Light on the surface, an undercurrent of darkness. Happens. Husband set in his ways, content. Wife, restless.

This couple had a strange and turbulent history, but were tight as porcelain on a bathtub. They had weathered terrible griefs to come this far. From an impossible crisis with their son, years back, they had surfaced. Battered, bruised, but triumphant, they had reached shore before the waves engulfed them. But

10

crisis was in the past and Cass had reached once again the limits of disillusion. And Galen, securely unaware, could not feel the heat, could not know of that disappointment that borders on the forbidden land of desperate action that had, of late, possessed his wife.

Cass knew that she was responsible for much of their problems. She had never settled into a regular job routine. Nine to five had appealed to her like a prison sentence. So, in recent years, she had tried free-lancing. She had failed at real estate and insurance. Now her enterprise was door to door in beauty and health aids. Powder and potions, as she described them. She made decent sales from time to time but was, due to flighty work habits, inconsistent. Cass knew that, with the kids grown, a solid job, even at the check-out counter, would be a tremendous help to Galen's long employment at the hardware store, seniority that never brought promotion. She marveled at the serene contentment of a man who had faced great danger.

Galen, oblivious to her thoughts, rose and walked to the living room. "Catch the news," he said. Routine, he said the same words every night.

In a sudden surge of utter confusion, loneliness engulfed the wife. Cass was suffocated by a blinding abandonment that paralyzed her throat, pressed her chest cavity with a breathless force. A thought surfaced . . . am I dying for my sins before I've even committed them? What power has grasped my brain, my lungs, my loins?"

Why did possibilities yet hidden deep bring back the small girl's fright she had always held at arms length? Why did the very notion of what she was toying with bring tremors, a journey into a black valley that, perhaps, she could not escape?

The abyss, the edge, why did it reduce her to this feeling of inadequacy, an inferiority she vowed to overcome? She had been there, years before, and had not only conquered the terror but, at the time, relished it, gloried in it. Those were the days of the mid-eighties when Galen had shown a flashing genius in a series of brilliant burglaries that raised the money to pay off the staggering debts that Andy's drug connections had laid on the supplier's back.

Cass had helped, had risen to the occasion. Did I run out the string, are we only allowed one segment of bravery and resourcefulness before falling back into the faceless crowd? I don't think so. Have a drink, it'll brace me up, even though drink can be a fearful adversary as well, an excess that must be controlled. Cass went to the fridge for a beer.

Who is there to share this with, if not Galen? When all is said and done, I can't burden Andy or Meg. I've nursed and disciplined and loved them all the days of their lives. I've felt their pain, exulted in their small triumphs. They are my life, my part of the bargain with human destiny to leave something better behind. I can burden them with my temper, my occasional irritability, my bossiness, all things par for the course.

But my dissatisfaction, my hunger for a bigger share of the pot, my sense of danger, of high dreams and adventure, they don't know of these hidden depth charges. There is no reason for them to ever know.

And friends. Some personal friends of the gentler sex – must I bring sardonic asides to these musings? All girl friends, old misnomers die hard. They are all fortyish women. Surely no matter how close, coffee klatch close, no matter how much they might love me, they could not keep a secret for as long as it takes to dial a phone. Nature would be dead against it.

The Criminal Housewife

Chapter 2

After dinner Cassandra and Galen Janes lounged in the living room. Coffee and cigarettes, nothing worthwhile on the cable box.

Galen Janes was preoccupied. Cass knew he was troubled, nothing to do about it until the inevitable interrogation. No hurry for that, merely a necessary process that needs enduring.

But Galen could not seem to gather his thoughts. He smoked a second cigarette, not a usual trait, more squirming than relaxing in that fake leather Lazy Boy. Next, thought Cass, comes the drumming of fingers. And so it happened. She waited patiently. If not tonight, some other time, what the hell's the difference?

"Honey, something's bothering me."

Cass was laconic. "Well, we've got three different laxatives in the med cabinet. Will any of them be of help?"

"Not at the moment. Naw, nothing wrong physically. I just sense, actually, that something is knawing at you. Am I correct?"

"Why don't you go to work for the Clinic? I hear they need good diagnosticians."

Galen went on, paying little attention. They had lived their years on velvet barbs.

"Come on, Cass, what's up?"

Sooner or later, she thought. We're alone. Meg is at work at her part time job at the fast food emporium. Call that a job? Andy, who had been home for the weekend, was back at the "U". Cassandra, in turn, lighted her second cigarette. These lousy tubes are killing both of us and we don't trust the T.V. public health ads on nicotine exposure. We don't want to trust them, I guess.

She said, "A little history, baby. Remember that summer a few years back when you went on that burglarizing and break-in spree?"

"Actually, I've forgotten."

She ignored this. "You, the most adept, innovative, clever criminal in the history of this area, raked in over ninety grand and the law never laid a glove on you. Not once."

"Pure luck."

"You were so damn good, you not only were never suspected, you were beyond suspicion and, in fact, a genuine hero on the jewelry job."

"I do faintly recall, now that you mention it. I like the hero part."

"Who wouldn't? And we ended up almost as broke at the end as when we started."

"Of course, we owed the drug establishment seventy-five grand on Andy's screw-up. I still figure we saved his life, the dumb asshole!"

"Galen!"

"Hey, easy. He was a punk kid then, not quite fifteen, both using and moving the stuff, and somehow it all disappeared. Now he's the greatest guy on earth. It was all worth it. Any more coffee?"

"Sure." She went to the kitchen for warm refills for both. "I don't intend to rehash all that ancient history. But remember what I said after we'd satisfied the debt, bought a different car and had just a few bucks leftover? I felt like a leftover myself. Used and abused."

"I remember. You were drunk as an English lord when you got on that stump."

"Sure I was drunk. Flying, as I recall. But, and here's the point, dead serious."

"I knew that. I figured you'd get over it."

14

"Gale, I did. To some extent and for a long time. But never completely. All that happened in the late eighties. Now it's 1995. I'm forty-four years old. I'm discontented. I have you and the kids so I shouldn't be. But, damn it, I am. Andy's gone, from the house at least. Meg'll be gone soon, she's fifteen."

"Happens to all families."

"I know, I know. And I shouldn't be different. But I am different. Not your fault, maybe not even mine. The genes thing, I suppose."

They regarded each other, almost as strangers.

Galen said, mildly, "Long time since we talked about the old days and what I – what we – were into then. But it wasn't for kicks or thrills. It was all just to save Andy from what? Knees shot off, that sort of thing. I was a bloody criminal, but I've never had a second thought."

"Me neither."

"But now, what're you talking about? Unless you'd rather keep your own counsel."

"I'm going back into business. Alone."

"Hmm. With what purpose in mind?"

This was the question she dreaded the most. She drew a deep breath and again refilled her mug.

"Greed. I won't dodge the word; why should I? I told you then that I wanted to be rich. For a few years I put the notion behind me. Behind, but never out of sight. Now it's back." She forced a laugh. "I have an itch to be rich. All my life I've more or less detested rich people. Mostly, I despised rich women. Rich bitches! Now I want to be one of them."

"You're aiming high, baby."

"A moon shot."

"So now you want to be a rich bitch. Beautiful." Galen shook his head, unreality was setting in. "How rich? Moderate, very rich or stinking rich? The category please."

"Moderate will do nicely, thanks."

"Thank God for that." Galen had little talent for irony.

This was his best shot.

"Of course," she murmured, "my own particular definition of moderate."

They smoked in silence, Galen on his third cigarette. A brooding quiet engulfed the room. I've been this route before, he thought. It's now role reversal time. Did I really, deep down, know that it'd come some day? Even so, how does a guy prepare? His gaze at his wife was a pure beam of adoration. They had met in high school, so many years ago. How many? Twenty-seven at least. He'd been smitten then and the feeling had never lessened. This lovely woman is more than my wife, she's my entire existence. I'll always need her, she sure as hell needs me right now. I've been to the ragged edge of crime. Cass hasn't.

His wife was troubled but, now, committed. She moved ahead, not easing up.

"I gave so damn much thought to this, hon," she said. "A hundred times I decided not to say a word to you. The accessory factor, you know. But, in the end, I couldn't. I'd bust a gut trying to shield a whole part of my life from you."

"I'll buy that. It's too great a burden on the system. Too much desolation. That can break the spirit. Do I dramatize?"

"Well, I couldn't confide in the kids. It'd tear up Andy, screw up his studies. Maybe, though, he could handle it. For sure, Meg couldn't."

"So," Galen forced a smile, "who but dear old Dad? Years ago I leveled with you on what I was about. Now?"

"I'll plunge ahead. I've come this far with you hon. And, of course, be it understood, no lectures, no second guessing."

"Of course not. I'm scared out of my wits by emancipated women. They terrify me. Me, a Nam Vet." A sudden weariness invaded him. The banter was great, but the underlying theme could scorch the soul. He had to know the worst, the scenario, no matter how insane.

Cass said, "I'll tell you what I'm about in planning these days. No sugar tit, straight up, a special operation at a special store."

"You got a gun?"

"Get real. No, a scam. Pure and simple, a rip-off. If I get away with it, and I shall. I feel invincible, Gale. I can't fail."

"Not a career change." She laughed, she also had a taste for irony. "Would I change my amazing career as advocate and counsel to the unbeautiful? Mary Kay would be devastated."

"I'm listening."

"One small scam. One big sucker, the granddaddy of the get-even syndrome. That's the whole program, folks. The big baby is in the future. A year, maybe, probably less. Maybe in four or five months."

"And for now?"

"Call this a warm-up. Training wheels, before I ride the big trail. Alone."

"Interesting, Who's the mark?"

"Dear old Boles Department Store. Supplier to the VIPS and the wanna bees."

"You have some animosity to Boles?" Galen could hardly believe the questions he was asking.

Cass laughed, she was feeling giddy. "Animosity! Where'd you pick up that word?"

"Actually, I know several, beyond my usual range of double syllables. And you're stalling."

"I guess. No, I like the store. Adds a bit of welcome class to our bourgeois town. But you've already answered, in your own mind, your own question. Because I've some sense of how your mind operates."

Galen merely waited.

"Well, two words will do nicely. Deep pockets. What else?"

"And legal resources beyond your imagination, Kid. In court - chew you up and spit you out. Pro against amateur."

"No way."

Again, Galen smoked impassively. He was now on number four. Old habit against an instinct that whispered to him of savaged lungs.

"The whole battle plan neutralizes the big advantage. We threaten big in court, we settle for less out of court. No legal record, no paper trail. And we get the figure we had in mind to begin with."

"Hmm. Aren't they on to all those tricks?"

"Of course, but they'll go along, we think. Stay out of court, play ball in the friendly confines of the office."

"Yeah? And, by the way, just who the hell is 'we'?"

"Your beautiful spouse. And, I think, Zack Taylor."

Galen was stunned.

"Zack? My old racquet ball buddy?"

"That's right. I don't know the man but I've done some research. Racquetball is as good an entry as any."

"That lying S.O.B. will tell you he usually beats me, if I know Zack. But you need a guy with some larceny in his soul." Now Galen laughed. For some indefinable reason, a small part of black despair had been lifted. "Zack Taylor. Well he's a dog, but, by God, it's all bulldog."

"And he'll be representing an innocent woman."

"Of course."

"My life is in your hands, Gale.. I'm glad you realize I had no choice but to level with you. I couldn't – couldn't bear the loneliness." Cass was suddenly losing it, almost babbling, the strain of holding back now released. "And, legally, I never told you."

Galen held her close.

"I promised you no lectures, Kid. I stick to my word." He kissed her lightly. "Good luck to you and Zack Taylor. I never dreamed I would be saying something like that."

"I don't need luck, Gale. Just losers rely on luck. All I need is skill."

"Famous last words, Kid."

"Anyway, as I've heard and you've told me, Mr. Taylor

is a personal injury specialist."

"And . . . ? "

"I'm about to be personally injured."

***

Walking through the beautiful upscale department store, Cassandra felt almost dream-like. She had imagined the scene so often that her actual presence now held all the ingredients of play acting, a substitute or even a dress rehearsal for reality. The aisles, the fixtures, lights and carpets were all physically present, real to the touch and feel and smell. An upper echelon store, Boles tolerated the average shopper, but set its sights upon those undulations of humanity that accepted only top drawer. Status heaven in a Midwestern city where price was unimportant, the brand name and quality, in lush surroundings, not only preferable, but necessary to status.

Cassandra was enveloped in this unreal feeling because a hundred imagined operations in the past weeks had drilled into her the actions of the automaton. She knew every inch, every nook and corner of display in the women's section so that she could have closed her eyes and never stumbled. Blinded, she could have touched each fur, each scarf and mohair sweater unerringly. Now the arduous training of physical movement and razor edge mind were to be tested. She was calm, a creature of ice and intelligence because she had prepared herself. No pulsing heart rate, no perspiration. Her face was bland and blank as the mannequins that populated this section of Boles, arbiter of taste and elegance in four hundred superstores across America. No deep breaths nor darting eyes.

There was no need to case again a situation she had waltzed through in countless imaginations and a dozen dry runs. I have done the home work, I have eliminated not only error but the very possibility of error. I am impregnable because, like a Knight of the Crusades, I have trained my body for the final, the thrilling, exhilarating test. So ran the thoughts of Cassandra Janes as she strolled, with magnificent abandon, the wide aisles of one of the nation's most prestigious stores.

Boles was at one end of the spectacular Cherokee Shopping Center, with the scenic, flowing Sarazen River nearby. Her husband, Galen, seldom shopped here, too pricey. Sears and Wards were more to his taste and billfold, not to mention the home building emporiums carrying everything from pole barns to wash pants.

Cassandra marveled at her own amazing calm. I knew I was meant for this, that I could handle it when the chips were down. Preparation, rehearsal, mental and physical, were the essentials. Like an actress walking through a stage role in a long running play, she thought, I have been here before, I know the lines and actions, I have the proper costume, my coat is comfortably bulky and below knee length.

She dropped to one knee as to retie a loose shoe lace, while her left hand darted into the open exhibit shelf and withdrew the wallet she had flashed into the display area. She slipped the wallet into her handbag, stood up and continued her leisurely saunter down the aisle. Cassandra felt invincible; the split second operation had gone exactly according to plan.

No hurry, enjoy the shopping spree, the furs, the gowns, the make-up – all the accessories of stylish comfort. She dawdled by a display of beautiful belts, peered at necklaces and rings – rings to suit the taste of a baroness, jewels glowing with smoky softness in the muted lights. Cassandra played out the string, walking slowly with all deliberate casualness to the front door, stepped out into the courtyard and felt, like an answered prayer, the light touch on her shoulder. She turned to face the plain clothes security man. Nice face she thought, a trim brown mustache, and the soft voice reciting the words honed in the manner directed to a hundred other suspects: "Madam, will you come with me, please, to the office? I'm sure I do not have to tell you why."

A withering look from Cassandra and a pulling away from the security man's touch. "You certainly do have to tell me why. I haven't the slightest intention of going anywhere with you." She looked around the courtyard, a few people, mostly women, were standing around. She raised her voice slightly, no hint of hysteria. "Just what is this bullshit?" The attention of the onlookers had been gained.

The handsome face was pained. The man had ten years of experience in this sort of reaction.

"Madam, we don't need any foul language. Just your cooperation. We know what we are doing."

Do you ever, thought Cassandra. What you are doing, you boob, is stepping right into the web. Thank you, sweetie, how did I ever luck into a nowhere clown like you? Way better than expected. She glared.

"You'd better know," her voice revved up another small notch. Cassandra recognized two of the women in the immediate area; they observed the scene with quiet interest. God, what luck, I couldn't have planted witnesses that I know . . . too risky. And, wham, here they are. "Very well, lead the way."

Together, they walked back into the store. They took the escalator to the second level and entered the plush general offices of Boles, Inc. Past the bored woman behind a reception desk and into a handsome private office behind.

The scene that followed played out in a nearly precise rendition of the many simulations that had coursed through Cassandra's mind in the days and weeks preceding. She was nearly in awe of the similarity. This is almost scary, she thought. I figured I was good, but this is beyond belief.

The charge was made by the security man. His name was revealed as Jack Veledez to the manager, a man in his early fifties who had earned his stripes though thirty years in the trenches in various Boles establishments throughout the country. He, also, was no stranger to such confrontations. Sticky fingers, and the cost resonates down to every item. These are the dregs of society, no matter how attractive, that drive up the cost for all of us.

The manager knew the litany, the sermon, by heart, as did all the managers, all officials, in the retail trade.

And so the charge was made and denied. Access to her handbag was demanded and scornfully granted, and the wallet, beautiful and stylish, was produced. The wallet, not a Gucci, but a near impersonation of that world-famous brand.

The wallet contained the personal driver's license, credit cards and other personal I.D. of Cassandra Janes, 407 Cravath Lane. "There is, also," said the aggrieved woman, "a sales slip at home confirming the purse had been purchased in Minneapolis six weeks earlier. The wallet was, in fact, exactly the same brand and type as those on the display at the local Boles, just slightly worn.

The case, within minutes, had been made, solid as concrete, and then demolished. The manager, William Adams, drawing from his years in the trade, knew exactly what to do. There was a scenario, company policy, that had always worked in the past. In the overall scheme of things, the zeal to protect the integrity of the merchandise and the open display theory of available goods, mistakes can be made. Once made, mistakes must be smoothed over.

Apologies followed, profuse and warm with good will and sincerity. An error on our part, Mrs. Janes, you are certainly free to leave, with our most profound regrets. Perhaps Madame would accept, as a token of friendship, a generous gift certificate.

"Ann," he said to the wide eyed receptionist, "make out a gift card for Mrs. Janes. Twenty-five - no fifty dollars - this is a valued customer." A genial laugh. "Good customers are our most precious asset."

Waving the gift offering aside, Cassandra took it all in steely grace. Politely she asked if she could use the telephone. She thumbed the directory and punched out the numbers. Meanwhile, Ann busied herself, offering Cassandra a chair.

"Thank you, dear," said Cassandra. Then, "yes, is this the secretary to Mr. Taylor? Yes. No, I cannot speak to anyone else. I see, I'll hold." Casually, she lighted a cigarette and waited. Mr. Adams busied himself behind his desk.

Cassandra smoked her cigarette in relaxation as she waited. Then, "Mr. Taylor, Zack Taylor? Yes, this is Mrs. Galen Janes. You don't know me, but you are, I believe, a friend of my husband. I think he has played racquetball with you at the 'Y'." She laughed, a rich, musical sound. "Yes, he says he beats you. Hey, does anyone ever lose? Oh," another laugh, "then he is the pigeon, not you?"

"The thing is, Mr. Taylor," she continued, "I'm at Boles department store. Yes. In the main office, second floor. I need you at once, it is vitally important." A pause, "Yes, I'll be right here. See you soon."

Cassandra flashed a brilliant smile at Jack Veledez and William Adams,

"Thank you," she said. "I'll just take a seat in the outer office until Mr. Zack Taylor, Attorney-at-law, arrives."

Adams paled visibly, but retained his poise.

"That isn't necessary, Mrs. Janes. An honest mistake has been made. One that could happen to anyone. We see no need for outside involvement."

"I'm sure you don't."

"Lawyers tend to make simple matters very complicated. I'm sure you are aware of that."

"I know nothing about complications. I have no idea what you mean. I simply know that a woman's character and name are her most precious possessions."

"Certainly."

"But that's just me. I know nothing about the law in such matters. One should always seek the advice of a professional, don't you agree?"

There was no reply to this. Adams and the security man exchanged glances. The conditioned air in the office was suddenly oppressive.

Cassandra finished her smoke, thumbed casually through a Boles catalog, then lighted another cigarette, staring blandly straight ahead, her jaw set. In fifteen minutes, Zack Taylor, attorney, arrived. He greeted Cassandra warmly.

After a brief whispered conversation, the four participants, Veledez, Adams, Cassandra and the attorney sat down together around the manager's desk and the lines were drawn in the first battle of the legal war against Boles, Inc.

The meeting lasted forty minutes, drawing to an inconclusive standoff. Cassandra and Zack Taylor departed with frozen dignity. Afterwards, William Adams sat at his desk, a feeling of inadequacy engulfing him. Adams was considered, in the trade, a merchandising wizard. He had battled his way from clerk to department head, assistant manager, then to the top spot at various Midwest cities in the Boles, Inc. empire. He loved buying and selling, knew the vagaries of business climates, knew the goods, women's wear, the men's department, sporting goods, crystal and sterling beauties, high on the list of bridal registries. Cosmetics, featuring the most expensive names from all over America and the Continent. Adams knew them all and hundreds of other lines, knew trends, fashion, administration.

If Adams had a weak spot, one that kept him from corporate headquarters, it was a less than perfect adaptation to people, both employees and customers.

Now this weakness threatened to upset, for the moment, his set routine, his expectations of daily grosses, always larger than those of the preceding quarter. He felt a pressure behind his eyes, something near to tightness around his heart. Decades of experience had given him some expertise in these matters, the spin verbiage to handle bothersome customers in a truly professional manner. Long days at headquarters workshops in the intricacies of cutting greedy customers down to size had given the harried manager some ability in these matters. Long tenure in such Midwestern strongholds as Des Moines, Wichita and Omaha, all tougher towns than this laid back farm town, had never faced him with a problem he could not, one way or another, handle.

Why, thought Adams, am I being plagued with doubts on this piddling matter, why this irritation, a feeling of being surrounded at this time? Stupid people in a stage coach town, he muttered, a bad joke. Was he intimidated by the even tempered aggressiveness of the plain speaking attorney, a man he instantly recognized as a rugged adversary, or the fact that the loyal security man, Valedez, could have handled the situation much better?

No. He knew, with a sinking feeling, that it had to be the woman. There had been no yelling, loud voices were a sign of weakness, easy to parry. The attractive woman, some local nobody, had composed herself with an easy dignity that hinted of wounds concealed, assaulted character controlled. William Adams knew, with a certainty of thirty years, that he was being had, that a velvet trap was closing around him. Much as he detested going "Upstairs," he would be forced to look for corporate rescue. His very being revolted against pleading to headquarters for assistance on a matter so trivial, so repugnant to his tailored sense of business righteousness.

These incidents were an annoyance. There is such a sense of excessive tort in the air these days, of grasping at straws to stick it to the establishment. But even though the case had all the outward signs of a truly formidable operation, in the end we will handle it. We have the legal manpower to close the books on this one without excessive cost and, most important, without the chilling factor of publicity. Mr. William Adams' confidence in the brilliance of Boles, Inc. legality was, despite the tightness in his chest, complete. After all, it would come down to this: a superb team versus one gold digger of a woman and her unsophisticated mouthpiece.

***

The late afternoon sun slanted in, highlighting dust motes in the spaces between the windows and the bar area. Dust motes denote living rooms and haylofts of youth, a peace that is impervious to change and modernism. Zack Taylor and Tom DeShales bellied up to the bar on high backed stools.

"If we didn't have this last resort to cling to in times of horrendous stress and malignant mischief, what would we have?" Not a question, really, just the rambling verbiage preceding a contented burp. Tom DeShales had digestive trouble that announced itself unbidden.

"Well, we'd still have the lake. And the golf course."

"Screw golf."

"You certainly do."

"Too damn much work. Course, fishing is work too. Hook on the trailer, drive to the lake, float the boat, etc., friggin cetera. But, at the end . . . ah peace. Even if the fish don't bite. Sometimes better if they don't."

"Don't what?"

"Bite. Are you listening?"

"Oh, sorry." Zack was, indeed, preoccupied, toying with a drink he usually made short shrift of. "But it's no problem."

"What isn't?"

Zack snorted. "Now who's listening? Pulling in fish. Just don't bait the damn hook."

"Sure. But I'm such a master fisherman I'd catch them anyway." DeShales waved languidly at the bartender for refills and tossed a twenty on the hardwood. "But the week has been a bobtailed bitch."

"Yeah?"

"That development out Cedar Creek way. Boy, that has looked great. Two acre lots, maybe forty, forty-five per. Plats out good, no trouble with utilities, no shit from the D.N.R. And plenty for the dear old legal toter of bales. Beautiful set-up. Too beautiful."

"Trouble in paradise?"

"Yeah. Well no, no trouble. No paradise. The financing went South, looks like no retrieval at this point."

"There's a million banks."

"Sure. And they all know how to say 'no dice'."

"Bummer."

The two friends worked on their Miller Lites. Both were beer drinkers, at least in the daytime hours. They figured, however erroneously, there was always a better chance of dodging a D.U.I. Stats didn't exactly bear out this theory but, no matter, they just liked brew.

"How're things in the whiplash department?"

"Slow. But I've got an interesting case coming up. Shop lifting. Or so alleged," offered Zack.

"Who got ripped off?"

"The big store. Boles."

"Boles, huh? Well, they're nation wide. No use stealing from Ma Perkins."

"That's what I say. Deep pockets. Deep down."

"Your client is innocent, of course?"

"Actually, she is. Better than innocent, she has a solid case, or so it seems, against false accusation, character assassination, hurt feelings. All that good shit."

"Has she got a character beyond reproach? Snow White and so on?"

"Pure white. Housewife. Works part time as a sales person. Beauty products. Zip record. One each hard working old man, two kids."

"Out of a sit com."

Zack sipped his Lite thoughtfully. He was relaxed, but troubled. DeShales pondered a perfect set up. Two hundred thousand dollar houses among the burr oaks and aspen swam before his eyes. That development had been a wondrous prospect, then the intrusion of reality.

"I think," said Zack, "I really think we are solid on this. But Boles has mouthpieces by the platoon, by the regiment. Still, mistakes are made, even by outfits that could buy and sell us out of petty cash."

"Well, I'm for sale."

"Hell, who isn't? If there ain't better things than work in this world, what's the point?"

"What happened?"

"She, Madame Client, stole a wallet. Not a Gucci, but about that pricey."

"And?"

"Stole the silverware, manner of speaking. But when they went back and counted the spoons, nothing missing."

"Some security guy screw up?"

"For sure. And that's surprising. An old hand. Been at the store-sleuthing racket for years."

DeShales grinned. An old fiction buff, he loved a touch of mystery and intrigue. Not always easy to come by in his specialty.

"So," said DeShales, "they catch your gal with the goods, but it's mistaken identity."

"It seems. But the mix-up was a beaut. She had a wallet in possession. But it was a look-alike, sort of, as I understand it. And it was hers, no question."

"This gets better."

"And yet better still. Security puts the arm on her as she exits the premises. But the wallet is hers. No case."

"You mean no case for Boles?"

"Exactly."

"But for the dishonored housewife and for your friendly, alert and intelligent barrister, a hell of a case."

"You forgot handsome."

"I'm lousy on summation," DeShales grinned. "Hey, Jackson, two more here. Zack is buying, I think. His turn comes every leap year, his counting."

"But," he continued, "do I detect the aroma that things never are what they seem? Do I detect, in my abject cynicism, the barest hint of, what delicate term should I use?"

"Try scam."

"Ah, yes, I am familiar with that treasured Latin expression."

"No chance." Zack pulled at his beer and squinted at the bar. "None. Zero."

"If such a chance existed, there is, of course, no way in which you could represent."

"Of course not." Pure sincerity was in Zack's voice. "I have my standards."

DeShales smiled. "Don't we all?"

"I'm just now getting into this case. Keep tuned to your friendly FM Station."

"I'll be all ears."

"May I remind you, so is a jackass."

"Where has the time gone? My beloved will have shoved my dinner in the fridge. If she ever prepared it in the first place."

"That being the case, and ditto for my happy household, how about another beer? Or two?"

"I like your math."

CHAPTER 3

Galen Wilbur Janes, for one of the first times in years, felt little comfort at work or at home. Peace of mind eluded him and it was not, entirely, the amazing scenario that Cass had laid on him a few days earlier. He had crossed the border from unreality to a frame of mind near to acceptance. He had, years before, schooled his wife in the subtleties of crime, albeit a different kind. A master of keys and locks, he understood burglary and was proficient.

But he had, long since, put all that behind him because the goal of those adventures had been accomplished. Now, the residue remained in a new and strange pattern, one that he could not begin to understand. This, to Galen, was a different breed, the whole syndrome of stealing, not by outright theft but by deception; the act of making your opponent – your "mark" – believe that what had happened had not, in fact, really happened. The act that convinced someone that damages must be forthcoming for an act too unbelievable to be fully understood even by those trained to ferret out deception.

Galen understood the risks, the long odds. But, in a moment near to shock, he had given his word not to interfere. His wife's life was her life, not his, no matter how intimate the bond. That she would lose, be prosecuted, disgrace the family, even be packed off to prison was not only possible, but likely. She told him once, years ago, that people were wealthy who didn't deserve good fortune. And poor, lower, middle, sometimes dirt poor, not for reasons either way, just the

31

random toss of some kind of celestial dice. Cass had many such notions, roughly gathered under the complex tent of maldistribution. She was, he had gathered through the years, a true and dedicated redistributionist, theories dating back to childhood and her wild six quarters at Madison in the turbulent days of Vietnam and the enhancing satisfaction of cannabis.

How long do the vapors, psychic and physical, reside in the lungs and bloodstream? Does a leopard change her spots or merely camouflage them until a future time?

This was his wife, for better or worse, mused the plain and thoughtful man. To desert her was unthinkable, to break a confidence beyond the borders of every impulse that made a man a man. A rueful smile. Cassandra is turned loose on an unsuspecting world. Let the world beware, you'll get no help from me. No warning, no sympathy, nor will Cassandra.

But the misadventures of his wife was not the only worry this late spring evening for Galen Janes. He faced his wife across the kitchen table and laid more pressure upon her because it was his family duty.

"Andy called me at work today."

"Yeah," she said, "he usually calls home."

"I know, this was between us. But he didn't specify keeping it from Mom."

"Well, that's something. Money trouble?"

Galen shifted uncomfortably. Outside of his long ago rescue of Andy from his dope connections, he had the common embarrassment of the working stiff with financial inadequacy. A wish, nearly a burning desire, to give his kids more than he had known himself. Things had not worked out that way. Galen and Cass had scraped up enough money to get Andy enrolled at the "U" and into halfway decent quarters. That was about all. "I can handle it from here myself," Andy had said quietly. And so he had, until now.

"Nearly a full time job. Thirty hours, often thirty-five

or more. Too much. He's finding he can't keep up the grades. Andy is smart, we know that, but the grind is tough. Two years to go, after this spring, six or more if he makes law school. Rough." Galen brooded. A man with no college himself, he still understood the vast gulf, the obstacles.

"I knew it, I just knew it," muttered Cass. "The poor kid was thin as a rail, last time home." She fired a cigarette without conscious thought. "Andy is too damn proud, said he could handle it alone. Hell, at what cost?"

"It gets worse. Andy is even talking of dropping out for a year or two, build up a bankroll. It's being done by a lot of kids, both boys and girls. Or, join the service, that would take care of his future education. If... "

"Yeah, if he ever went back. And it's four years, too long, too big a slice."

"I'm tapped out, more or less," said Galen. "But I can raise a couple bills, maybe three or four, and I will. But what's a few grand against that mountain if we intend to have him cut down on the outside labor?"

"We'll work it out. And don't forget my special project." Cass murmured this, half in jest.

"Cass, your special project doesn't exist as far as I'm concerned. You're out on a limb so far we can't program it into any plan." Galen, in honor of his pledge, spoke evenly. Inwardly, he seethed. What insanity was entering his home, his family? And could they forever shield this new direction from their children?

"The children," almost to himself. "Of course, they're not children anymore. They're two wonderful adults." Cass did not interrupt him. He went on. "On this matter, you've always been way ahead of me, baby. They will be gone, somewhere. Their own homes, families, jobs, trades, professions, whatever. I have no brothers or sisters, nor do you. Our parents are long dead. The past is all buried. How did we manage to become so alone?"

"We didn't 'manage' hon. Turn of the cards. Some people get twenty-one dealt, others get thirteen and bust. The blackjack example isn't perfect, but the Indian Casinos invade my thoughts. Fortunes made, by a few, fortunes lost by many, including some elected officials."

Now Cassandra was brooding, mirror image of her husband. "My enterprise is off the board for conversation. So we've agreed and so it shall be. But on percentages I'll take it over the cards or dice, forget the one arm bandits. And Andy's needs have a big place in the whole picture, my view."

Galen did not answer. He was drawn, powerfully, to dissent, to argue, to point out once again the terrible dangers of his wife's chosen path. But any answer, no matter how cold and impersonal, could lead to shouts and recriminations. Hands off the deal, he would go the distance. With a stoicism, key to his nature, hardened in the fires of Vietnam, this gentle working man would play his destined role. He would report, five days a week, plus until noon on most Saturdays, to his ingrained job at Cardinal Hardware. No bed of roses, no crown of thorns. Just another day, another few dollars, dull as dirt in a basic industry. He felt, suddenly, old. Weariness engulfed his entire being. Galen was ready for bed but new surprises awaited him.

"Gale, I must tell you this. What I have planned and talked about is now more than a fancy theory."

"I don't follow."

"The plan. The operation, the first phase, has already been put into operation."

"Into operation? I'm lost."

"We talked about Boles as the lucky participant, the unsuspecting accomplice in all this."

"Your first choice, as I recall."

She grinned now, a sardonic and mischievous smile. "Yes, number one. I wonder if the folks at Boles appreciate the honor."

Galen waited.

"The operation was carried out a few days ago. Been waiting for the right opportunity to tell you."

"I've been here."

"I know, God, I know. But, actually talking to you, the operation was easy, in comparison."

Galen, thunderstruck, fought for composure. Planning, talking, had been a wild pipe dream. Now this. Cold reality.

"Don't tell me the details, Cass. I'm not sure I want to know."

"And I'm not sure you should know."

"What follows?"

"Zack Taylor follows."

"Oh yeah, Zack."

"Zack Taylor, hack lawyer and sometime racquetball player, and your lovely wife are working it out."

Galen exploded. "Working it out! What's to work out? The local paper, all the damn media, will stage a circus on this."

"Not true."

"The newspaper is in the news business, happens to be their job. They'll drag us in. I don't care about myself, but Meg and Andy, what will it do to them?"

"Calm down, hon. And listen."

"OK. I'm listening."

"I told you before. No one will know. You think publicity is bad for us? For Boles, it's poison," Cassandra explained patiently. "Think about it from their point of view. You know, the customer base."

"That your intelligence from Taylor?"

"Intelligence! You sure hang on to those old chestnuts from the Army. Natural, I guess, after what you went through. God, Galen, when I think about those days. You were just a kid yourself, younger than Andy is now."

"That was then, this is today."

"Sure. And you're partly correct. Taylor does agree, it's the basis of our whole strategy, except he thinks I'm innocent. No, the decision is mine. I know it will work, everything will be done in secret, far from the maddening crowd."

"That's 'madding,' if you're quoting the poet."
"What the hell."

The Criminal Housewife

CHAPTER 4

The poker game, a twice a month ritual, had come and gone. Four other players had departed the DeShales paneled basement. Empty beer cans littered the green felt table and crumbs from Mrs. DeShales sandwiches, offered in stony silence, had managed to reach the carpet.

Zack Taylor and Tom DeShales were poker buffs, as were the dear departed, another attorney, two independent businessmen and a retired cop. Various other types filled in from time to time as vacations and other matters interfered. The playing style of the two friends mirrored their lifestyles. Tom, deliberate and careful, seldom bluffed, usually won. Zack played with an erratic disdain for the law of averages. Alternately, he won big or lost a bundle.

The game itself, evolved over the years, was neither big nor small. Ten dollar limit, three raises. Some split pots, mostly straight. No limit had been tried at one time but discarded as too rich for a regular diet. The ten limit left a certain margin for bluff and kept bad luck from being catastrophic on any given sitting. In the evening's proceedings, both men were, for one of a rare number of sessions, winners. Tom DeShales had coolly and very conservatively coaxed his cards to a seventy-five dollar win. Zack Taylor had blustered and battered his way up and down the range, even cashing a check at one time, but closed with a flourish and one forty-five plus. So, no wounds to nourish, no second guessing to trouble the brain cells.

Now, past one A.M., a nightcap was called for. Contrary to the brewery custom, Tom had tapped a liter of Old Granddad and they sipped the amber stuff straight up.

"I don't like to pry" said Tom.

"Since when?"

"I ain't that bad."

"Shit, you could write a book, a whole shelf of books on other peoples' cases."

"Natural curiosity. I have deep feelings for the human family in all its twists and vicissitudes." He yawned. "You should be flattered I take an interest in your mundane matters."

"I am. Flattered and passionately grateful."

"Then, what gives?"

"You are referring, I assume, to the continuing adventures of Cassandra?"

"Yeah. And I love that name."

"Well," Zack had a wicked glint. "To me, just Cass. We're tight."

"What happened to client objectivity?"

"It's a thing people preach. They don't practice it, not with blondes."

DeShales sipped his whiskey and regarded his old friend fondly. "Progress. For me. We've determined her hair color. Your progress is of a road less traveled."

"Naw. I'm behaving. Soul of discretion. Besides I have a feeling she'd deck me in a minute if my fly slipped a notch on the zipper. I was kidding."

"Tell me more. This strikes me as a hell of a case,"

"The woman's bright, articulate and, of course, mad as hell about the invasion of her integrity. She's got the fire in her belly to see this thing through."

"Winnable?"

"Not the slightest doubt about it."

"Filed yet?"

"No." Zack got up and walked around the table, trying

to focus his thoughts. "We're in the talking stage. But a filing seems inevitable at this time."

"How heavy?"

Now the voluble Zack was quiet for minutes. He refreshed his drink and studied the fake flames in the fake fireplace. Perfect, he thought. What isn't fake these days? Fire that does not burn. As long as you pay the gas bill.

"This just between you and me?" Zack broke off. He knew he had proposed the ultimate insult to his pal.

"Sorry Tom. That just slipped out."

"It's OK. Forget it."

"I mean, if we can't tell each other stuff like this..."

"Yeah, what price friendship? Or cellmates?"

"I think, half a mil."

DeShales whistled, a startled sound between his teeth. "If it doesn't date me, cool."

"But it's just conversation at this time."

"Of course. Fall back?"

"I dunno, but I think possibly two hundred and ten grand."

"Hmm. Interesting. Mind telling me the thought process involved here?"

"Not at all. It's mostly hers. Cassandra, that is. Her thinking. Two ten, divided by thirds. One forty for the client, seventy for me. It's neat, tidy. Easy math, the kind I can handle."

"But you're the expert. According to your shingle." Zack smiled. He was getting a bit drunk so no hurry to leave until he burned off some of the alcohol.

"My client has this drill she's adapted. Must have read it somewhere. Maybe T.V., who knows where people get their notions?"

"Drill?"

"Naw, not drill exactly. I was searching for the right word. More like a grand design."

"I'm lost. Not for the first time with you."

"I struggle not to be obtuse."

"Balls!," DeShales laughed. He, too, was feeling the warmth of ninety proof. Relaxation invaded all his joints. He loved the give and take, the banter of pure bullshit. "Can your struggle bring you to the point of elucidation?"

"Cassandra, my client, is fixated on three words, three little words, and nothing to do with love. They are, in no particular order, awardable, appealable and collectable." Zack grinned wickedly. "Great words from one of the unwashed masses."

"She out of soap?"

"Figure of speech, the lady is immaculate. And not without a smattering of education. She went to Madison for a year or two back in the late sixties, early seventies, somewhere in there. Mostly to protest the war and raise hell, I guess, while her old man was in Nam."

"Pre law?"

"Naw. But what's the difference? Everybody is a lawyer today. Like I said, all those T.V. shows."

"Well," muttered DeShales. "With those three words, your bombshell has her head screwed on right."

"Let me guess," he went on. "See how far off I am. The client has an idea how much she can possibly get. Either negotiation or a court award. Thus, awardable. But too large an amount, the storm flags go up from the Boles Corporation, partly because of the dollars, partly because of our old pal, Mister Precedent. The other two words are twin sisters. If an award is appealed, it takes months, years to collect, if ever. A more modest sum (the word modest is a stretch where Zack Taylor is concerned) is perhaps, even likely, collectable because of 'What the hell, we can't jack around with this piss ant case all year, not to mention the killer publicity.'"

Tom DeShales grinned. "How'm I doing, defender of the faith?"

"One hundred per cent. You're in the wrong line of the noble profession."

"How'd your gal, Cassandra, get so smart? I mean

discounting preplanning? Is she a 'natural' like some of those ballplayers?"

"That, my friend, is a puzzling question. One I have pondered exceedingly. And one that, in the final analysis, I don't give a damn about."

"Nor I."

"Man, it's getting late. Later than you think in the big picture, but no philosophy for me tonight."

"Hmm, well drink up. Then get the hell out of here. I've got a big fight tomorrow with Planning and Zoning. And who knows how many knock downs, go to a neutral corner, with the old lady?" A heavy sigh, "OK, Lord, is there no end in sight for my travails?"

To this complaint, Zack Taylor offered no comment. He was painfully aware of the tribulations that DeShales encountered at home. Shirl, the wife in question, was a striking, high spirited woman of ravenous appetites and a zest for adventure far beyond the norm for an attorney's helpmate in a mid-size, conservative snow belt city. How does the man cope, thought Zack. My wife, with all her burdens, our burdens, of a handicapped son, is an amazing gal. She guides me with a rein so light I hardly feel the leather.

But the card games, the fishing, the hunting, all help. We all need a balanced life, a noble goal. Unattainable, of course, but with a wife of unpredictability and wild mood swings, the balance becomes increasingly beyond reach, the dangers of confrontation, greater.

"Long night's journey into day, buddy," said Zack. "See you, whatever."

"Good night, Zack," said DeShales. You might be in for a great season. The paper says personal injuries up six percent."

The Criminal Housewife

CHAPTER 5

The two attorneys met for lunch the day following the
poker game. Just cheeseburgers and cokes in a fast food
emporium. Both men liked to eat light, if not sensibly, at
midday. Warm sunshine enveloped them in their
southern booth exposure. Golfers and outdoorsmen,
they did not shrink from old sol.

"Never asked you last night, we got too bleary," said
Tom DeShales, "and maybe you'd rather not go into it.
But I'm fascinated. Just what was the nuts and bolts of
the whole bit that led up to your client's – hey, your
client's and your – decision to go after Boles."

"Well, of course I wasn't there, came in later, you
know. But I got a pretty clear picture of just how it all
came down from both parties."

"The fair Cassandra and the security guy?"

"Of course. Mrs. Janes, Cassandra, was on one knee
at the time."

"Huh?"

"Tying her shoelace."

"O.K. Then?"

"The security man says he thought she reached out
and snatched a wallet from the open display. She says
she might have put out her hand to steady herself, put
her hand on the edge of the rack."

"But no heist?"

"Heist? Your vocabulary is worse than mine. Where
did you come up with that dinosaur?"

"I dunno. T.V., love those cop shows. And I read a lot.

A lot. Centerfolds – the - whole bit."

"I'm so inclined myself, truth be known. But no, no heist. Nothing."

"What happened in the office after the pinch?"

"Red face time. Huge red face time. They commandeered her hand bag, had to practically grab it from her. Opened it..."

"And," surmised DeShales, "Voila, nothing there!"

"Not quite. A beautiful wallet. Almost Gucci quality. Pretty much like the ones on display."

"Balls, this is interesting. Sounds like dead to rights." Zack Taylor scoffed.

"Dead to nothing. Cassandra's wallet was two months old. Stuffed with all her own crap. Personal, driver's license and so on. She'd bought the wallet in Minneapolis, the Boles store up there. Still had the sales slip at home."

DeShales was beyond surprise. He shook his head like a man fighting the bends.

"I'll be – was there, what, testimony, collaboration, whatever, from any store camera?"

"Sort of. Not too clear. The camera showed Mrs. Janes dropping to one knee, and kind of a flash, it's indistinct, of her arm grabbing the display case to steady herself. Not a good picture at all, partly because of her bulky coat."

"Then what happened?"

"Way I get it, The Boles people, manager and the security guy, Veledez, Jack Veledez, were stunned. Freaked out of their minds."

"Yeah?"

"Yeah. Freaked out, big time. They had the perp. Little Miss Sticky Fingers right in the cross hairs. Absolute. Then, wham bang, they had nothing. Zero, empty chamber."

DeShales nodded.

"Nothing? Seems to me they had a hell of a lot less than nothing. Nothing plus a mess of catfish they can't clean."

"You bet, Nada. Somebody snapped the steel trap, but the beaver was gone."

"Speaking of stunned, your alliterations are stunning, if, perhaps, unconscious."

Zack ignored this.

"The Boles people, I guess all the folks in the department store gig, get a little paranoid. Understandable. I would, too, in their shoes. They get ripped off a lot. School kids snatch lipsticks, candy, panties, any damn thing. Gets old."

"I'm sure."

"But it won't fly. It's no excuse, absolutely no damn excuse for putting the arm on an innocent person, a nice woman like Mrs. Janes."

DeShales finished his coke and grabbed both cups. He headed for the beverage bar and scored refills for both. He looked at his friend long and hard after returning to the booth. He was troubled.

"Still" he said.

Zack Taylor was suddenly all business, a reversal from his usual laid-back casualness.

"Don't say it, Tom. Just, goddamnit, don't say it."

"I wasn't about to say...

"I know. But that word 'still.' There's just a woman who has been maligned, insulted, degraded – witnesses are available and eager, if necessary. There is nothing beyond that. Nothing. I go with the situation as presented to me. As is. And I share the facts with my buddy, that's you."

"Sure."

"The world is full of deceit. Fishy deals, scams, dishonesty, rip-offs, stuff you and I haven't even dreamed of, my learned friend. I'm, at heart, just as much a skeptic as you. Maybe more. It's my nature and the characters I've been exposed to in my kind of practice."

"Hey, Zack. Cool. I slam you as the whiplash lord.

Same as you dig me on Shangri-La developments that might as well actually be in Tibet. It's bullshit, fun and games to keep our sanity in this weird profession."

Zack Taylor sipped from his refill and gazed fondly at the other man. They were in their middle forties, both with scraggly careers and contrasting marriages, second for each. But they had that indefinable miracle that helps and heals, that makes life interesting and worthwhile. They had friendship.

"Thanks, buddy. I need the money but I don't take cases unless they pass the odor test. This one does – spring flowers and Liz Taylor perfume all the way. Otherwise, I wouldn't be aboard."

DeShales winked. "Did my faith in you and human nature stutter for just one moment there? Hell, it's back."

"I'm obliged."

"I don't know as much about Boles as I should. Hardly keep up on all that Fortune 500 stuff even though I know I should."

"I'm no authority on them myself. I don't have to be for this issue."

"But big. Real big?"

"One of the half dozen largest retailers in the nation. Big in revenue, huge on Wall Street. Somewhat smaller than General Motors. A bit larger than Rhode Island. That's all I know. I own no stock in this outfit. Or General Motors. Or IBM. I just own dogs. I buy a stock, it goes down. Fact of nature. You want a corporation to go belly up? Easy. Just induce Zack Taylor to buy some stock. Kiss of death."

DeShales chuckled. He liked to get his pal going on the soap box. He loved his friend for himself but, just as much for the entertainment value. Zack, crude and somewhat a slob, had depths of insight beyond many other professionals. Or so believed Tom DeShales, attorney, whose own career in real estate was beleaguered and whose marriage was hanging by a thread. Without Zack Taylor, tough times would be almost impossible to endure.

"Surely, an interesting case, to put it mildly," said DeShales. "But you've got to get me zeroed in on the main dish."

"If you're not talking money, I don't know Tom DeShales."

"I am speaking of the filthy commodity," he smirked. "As I expect you are."

"You got that correct. But all in good time. We haven't proceeded that far yet. I might even need your advice, no billable hours, on that part."

"How about five minutes from now?"

"Nice offer. I counter with a few days. By that time, I'll know up from down."

"Sure. I'm joshing, not pushing. But my mind is swimming with financial arrangements, financial hopes, dreams, expectations. All that happy green paper that keeps the wheels greased and pays the gas bill."

"Well, I've got my ideas. But, and this is one huge caveat, my client may have different ideas altogether. She's pretty hot. Don't take that throwaway wrong."

"Never."

"Point is, at the moment, she's a volcano ready to blow. A woman scorned. Like that."

"I would think so."

"But we'll make progress, a meeting of the minds will follow. You can be sure."

"You're a gambler, Zack. Sort of. You don't play poker as well as I do but you're OK. Practice law, play poker, blackjack, all the same. A gamble."

"Our sainted profession aside, you can't put them in the same category. Poker is one thing, blackjack quite another."

"What are you saying? Like football is one game, baseball another. That's profound."

Zack paid no attention. "Poker is against other players, your friends, even birds if you're lucky enough to have a pigeon or two in the game."

"We get birds in our regular game. Buzzards."

"What I mean is, it's against other guys. Like in a lawsuit. Bluff and counter bluff."

"But in the end you have to have the goods. You can only bluff so much with dud cards."

"Exactly."

"I forget what point you were making," said DeShales, wearily. This happened often.

"Blackjack is entirely different. You can't bluff your fellow players. It's like they don't exist. They're just sitting there like you. And forget the dealer. Doesn't matter if it's a smart mouth guy or a knockout blonde."

"Matters to me."

"Well, it shouldn't. The dealer is there to just pull cards out of the shoe, one by one."

"Fours and sixes to you. Backed up face cards to the dealer. Or worse, face, ace."

"Seems like it."

"You play much, Zack?"

"Naw, can't get away. Three nights in Vegas a fortune. Local Indian casinos, not too glamorous. You?"

"I always get clipped like a sheep in April, so I quit." DeShales yawned. "You finish your lecture, professor?"

"Just starting. We've agreed the dealer is unimportant, just a prop, could be a machine. Has to hit sixteen, can't hit seventeen. Although in some casinos they are allowed to hit soft seventeens. I stay away from that action completely."

"Makes a small difference."

"Anyway, to get on with this, poker is an activity where you are pitted against human nature. Blackjack is against statistics. And the stats say you can't win in the long run. They got any more coffee in this joint? Mine is like ice."

"The coffee does not run dry, my friend, nor does your golden throat, may I be so observant." DeShales went to the counter for refills and sprang for the cost.

"Therefore, forget the other players, the dealer, the gal with the drinks. Pit your brain against the stats. Don't bust yourself, let the dealer bust. And double up when you're hot."

"Won't work."

"I know. But neither will the alternatives."

DeShales shook his head in wonderment. "Lousy stocks, bad real estate, witch of a woman. Figured I had a lock on every way to go broke, now I have the new blackjack twist. More death by attrition. I should have been a cat. Last longer, by a multiple of nines."

"Not alley cats."

"You talking about me or my wife?"

"Just an observation for cripessake. Words of wisdom gleaned from a lifetime of trial by fire. Don't personalize it."

"How about craps, payday pastime of G.I.'s for a hundred years?"

"Not a bad gamble and lots of action if you don't mind standing up 'till you're broke. But again, for us, only in Vegas. No crap tables at the local native American sweatshop. A shame."

"Takes three men to run the game. They all have to be paid. Must be something in it for the house to handle that bite."

"Has to be in the odd bets. Pass or don't pass, the little dots on the cubes are the same for everyone. But the cubes have never been kind to me."

"And you're such a deserving fellow."

"I know."

"What about slot machines?" DeShales was probing further. "The one armed bandits?"

"Are you sick?"

"I know a guy hit five grand on the bandits at one of the Indian pits."

Zack was incredulous. "You know a guy. I know a guy. Everybody knows such a guy. So the hell what? We also know a hundred guys stick their whole paycheck in the bandits, or their kissing cousins, the pulltabs, every week. And forget the damn groceries and shoes for the kids. They build beautiful casinos on those electronic marvels. They build on losers, not winners."

"You are so right, buddy. The question was arbitrary and capricious. Also out of order, the jury is instructed to disregard."

"Speaking of juries, a good lot to avoid, if humanly possible. Unpredictable."

"Yeah. Another part of the gamble."

"We're all licensed to practice this strange occupation. We should be licensed as professional gamblers, amounts to the same thing."

"Well, you've got the wind up, bit in your teeth, all that old malarkey on this case."

"The bastion of Boles shall fall." Zack was confident. "Still it's a gamble. Eight to five on the big board."

"That's good action." DeShales rose to leave. "Good luck to you and the lovely Cassandra."

The Criminal Housewife

CHAPTER 6

Cassandra and Galen, for a change of pace, enjoyed a night on the town. Dinner and drinks at Michelle's, one of the attorneys' favorite spots. But no lawyers, at least none they knew, were in sight. A quiet mid-week evening in a spot that showered memories on them from younger days.

Actually, it was Cassandra's doing, the celebrating. Galen, reserved, as always, was along for the ride. "I'm buying," his wife had announced at home. "You've been grabbing the check for all our married life. My turn, baby. Makes me feel a little less of a drone. Or a bought lady. How much am I worth tonight ... ten bucks, ten thousand?" On she bubbled, Galen had not seen her so deliriously happy in a long time. How do you refuse a gift of steak and cocktails from a gal like that?

But he could not keep his mind from the subject that had dominated the past weeks. Galen found himself at a crossroad, not involved yet, beyond each breath of his life, concerned for Cassandra.

"I bought a pair of slacks today at Boles. Couldn't find what I wanted at Penney's or Sears."

"Gray, I assume."

"What else?"

"Judas, Gale, anything else. You've bought gray slacks since we were in high school."

"In Nam I had a distinct change of color and style. Remember? Uncle didn't feature gray."

This is not a good sign, thought Cass. When Nam

comes back, like an old haunting, I know his mind is disturbed. Always happens. "Sure, I remember, hon, how could I forget? And you looked smashing in those godawful army duds. Good looks'll do it."

"Point is, Boles seems to've weathered whatever you and Zack Taylor are plotting against them."

"You worried about the bottom line on Boles' annual report?" Cass' sarcasm was flowing in full measure, with the Margaritas providing the lubricant.

"Naw, what's a few digits to that outfit. Just concerned about the price of pants, socks, underwear – all that glamorous merchandise." He caressed her arm, the mighty Margaritas hitting his bloodstream also.

"Big numbers are for another time, another place, hon. Chump change, as Zack says, on this little caper. We crawl before we can walk, before we can run. You know how it goes, Big Daddy, like when the kids were babies."

Galen motioned to the raven-haired waitress. "Another round, Vi."

To Cass, "last round for me and I hope for you. Might need a taxi, as is. I fired the designated driver tonight, so it might be sober cab for the Janes'."

"I've seen the time when I might challenge you on the drink limit. Not tonight. I've become a tough, disciplined soldier in my own army."

"Your army?"

"Yeah. A striking force of one. I'm the general, major, buck private – the works. I conquer or am conquered on my own merits. Into the Valley of Death rode the lone trooper."

"You're hamming it up, Kid."

"Why the hell not? The whole business is a battle of nerves and mine are holding up like a steel brassiere on an old movie queen."

"Cute."

"Oh, hell, Gale. I'm celebrating victory tonight. That's why I'm throwing this bash, just for us. I want you to be as happy as I am."

"I don't know exactly what victory we're toasting. You haven't clued me in lately."

"I know, hon. Things dragged on for some time. Then wham, you win, Ma'am."

"Fill me in."

"We won, baby. Not on substance, but on style. We pleaded without begging. We threatened by innuendo. I don't think Mr. Taylor and I had the power or resources to blacken the Boles' name in this section of the state, if we were denied satisfaction, but somehow we convinced them we could ruin them. I still can't believe the amazing bluff that Taylor can run. Must be all those late night poker games with that gang of cutthroats he hangs with."

"So?" Galen Janes drew a huge sigh of relief. He felt a new freedom. "It's all over then?"

"The check is cashed and in the bank, one hundred forty strong men for your brilliant wife. Seventy for our favorite Shylock."

Galen was too numb to respond, his system drained.

"And," added Cass, "I'm as fresh and unspoiled as Rebecca what's her name, the one from Sunnybrook Farm. There is no record in any Courthouse file, no paper trail. Everything was settled without involving his honor or her honor or those twelve flint-eyed folks in the jury box."

"You goofy screwball. I don't know whether to laugh or weep like a child. You are either damn smart or damn lucky. Maybe both."

"Luck beats brains, even at the crap table."

Galen, in a sudden rush of affection, held her right hand in both of his. This lovely, vibrant woman was his wife and she was, after a strange odyssey, safely back.

"When this started, you know what I thought – "

"That I was crazy as a hoot owl in heat and a solid candidate for the Big House."

"More or less. But thank God, it's all over. Even if I

still have a few, what the hell's the term, moral reservations, I guess."

Cassandra looked at him, a level gaze. "Nothing is over, you know that, hon."

"What do you mean?"

"I explained all this at the beginning. This was a camel's nose under the tent. Training wheels, boot camp."

A painful stab entered Galen's stomach where a joyful feeling had been. He knew, in an instant, that Cass was dead serious, the long travail of worry and suspense would begin anew.

"I know, Cass, I know. But I figured that if – if you put this deal to bed safely, you would thank the stars that watch over you and wrap it up."

Cassandra, though well enclosed in a mellow mood, was suddenly out of patience.

"You figured wrong, friend. And, for the record, you are my dearest, most adored friend, remember that. But I jumped aboard the bandwagon for the big stash. One-forty? – you gotta be joking. The next deal is for the jackpot, pull that lever and let the silver coins rain down, baby." She was now in full flight. "Can't you remember, Gale, or don't you <u>want</u> to remember? You pulling a black-out on me?"

Galen was deliberate. "I know what you said. I didn't believe it because it wasn't possible. I still feel the same."

"Well, no matter. It's all systems go."

"I don't want to lose you, Cass."

There was real anguish in the words. Cassandra's natural tenderness returned.

"You won't lose me, hon, no chance. I've found this talent, this ability to accomplish what I first started out to do. To be a rich bitch. Remember?"

"You're getting awfully close to being a drunken bitch, if I'm any judge."

"I know it. And ain't it beautiful?" She giggled into her empty Margarita.

Galen pondered. He had truly expected this, but had hoped against hope that he was wrong, that a sea change had ensued from the one-forty. Now, filled with the liquid glory of Margaritas he was, nevertheless, bitterly disappointed. Was there a recent movie or book called 'Whose Life Is It Anyway?' Life imitating art was at the doorstep.

"My pledge is still good, Cass. I never go back on my word. But I have to be honest. I wish you'd pack it in."

"No chance."

"That being the case, what's your next move? Where will the good doctor operate now?"

"I've been thinking about that. Not the location, that's fixed in my mind. Just whether I should share it with you. I've got a gut feeling, hon, you really, truly, don't want to know."

"You may be right. Yeah, I'm positive you're right. Ignorance is bliss and I'm as ignorant as they come." Galen tried to keep the patter light, but a touch of real bitterness was in his voice.

"Hey, baby, lighten up. Look at it this way. I keep my promises, too. And the next operation will be my last. Guaranteed."

"Hm - guarantee, warranty, what the hell, your word is sterling silver. It's not a lot of relief, but it's some. Wives always lie to the old man, so I've been told, but not you. Near as I know," he grinned. "I guess you're right, I really don't want the details, not sure my ticker could hack it. But how about an approximate time frame? I can only hold my breath so long."

"Understood. Well, I've got to catch breath. But not too long. I have to ride this fine edge of nerve before I lose it. Fevers flare, fevers recede."

"You're talking pretty esoteric for a dangerous woman. But you're not answering my question."

"I can't, hon. You only asked for approximate so I'll throw in this figure. Within the next two or three months. O.K.?"

Galen smiled. "Not O.K. – but O.K."

The die had been cast for both the immediate and future decisions. No use backing off now. Another round of Margaritas were ordered and blissfully downed.

Then, the conference over, Galen walked to the pay phone, listing slightly to the right. A call brought a fast response and a driver for Checkerboard Cab appeared within five minutes. "We'll leave the car in the lot, love. Pick it up tomorrow morning. With all you've got on your platter, we can't complicate it with a D.U.I. for me."

Fighting back from the swirling winds of alcohol, Cass, iron willed, agreed. Galen marveled at the easy manner, the straight walk of this remarkable woman, reborn into his gray existence. It is gray, he thought, and uneventful. Just like my slacks.

The Criminal Housewife

CHAPTER 7

Following the Boles' settlement, Cassandra, feeling free as a bird on the wing, used the golden days of August and September to plan and scheme for the wars of the coming months. In her preparations she actually drew her tactical moves out on paper. The strategic campaign, deployment of forces, she told herself, had long been determined. As she had informed her husband, Cass had zeroed in on the preferred target. The objective is definitely in my gun sights; I just need the exact flight plan, no deviation allowed.

And so, in the military allusions she still retained from Galen's army service, she planned and devised – and shopped.

The one-forty (the amount she had ridiculed to Galen) was, in fact, a heady bankroll. Andy and Meg must be provided for immediately and better than in the past. Galen's castle, this average home, needed serious improvement, for their existence if they stayed, for more lucrative resale if they moved. She spent many hours in consultation with roofers and furnace people. In these exploratory meetings, Cassandra bargained tough, she perfected the casual walk away if she detected the faintest hint of future gouging. I harvested this dough the hard way, she reasoned, and there will be much more to come. I can easily justify my actions. I'm the mother bird and the little open beaks in the nest are hungry, but I'm not earth mother to the rest of the city.

She visited car dealers, not to make an immediate

choice, but to draw a bead on the future. Caddies, Lexus, Mercedes, Lincolns, the luxury vehicles were the only ones that piqued her interest. I've put in my time on this earth with Fords and Plymouths. No put down to them, they're great cars, but I'm gonna ride this wave of easy money in a set of wheels that will strangle the eyeballs of the neighbors. She examined the sleek, expensive cars, slammed the doors and kicked the tires, but she did not commit.

The budget stores, Target, Shopko and Wal-Mart that she had haunted through the years were now off the charts. Lovely stores, she murmured, but this family is moving on up. So long bargain counters and Wednesday sales, nice knowing you. And so she shopped long and carefully for Meg but, in the end, bought nothing. When I was fifteen, I wouldn't have been caught dead in what my mother would buy me. Can't be done, that's why my high school days were spent in the bleached jeans and pullovers, whatever I could scrounge.

Meg was impressed when her mother revealed all this to her. Never overly concerned with clothes, she, nevertheless, liked to look something other than a tomboy at school. She happily used her mother's financial guarantee to apply for and receive her own open door to freedom, a credit card.

"I won't abuse it, Mom. Promise." Meg could hardly contain herself. The girl's whole life was not bound up in her charitable work and she envisioned a classy new outfit from a store such as Boles.

"Honey, I know that. You're the most unselfish kid I know. Just don't overdo the conservative. I want you looking great. You deserve it."

"I don't know about that, Mom. But the cost. I just won't run up big bills for my clothes. We can't afford it."

Cassandra laughed, it was so gratifying to be able to laugh at such talk.

"Sure, you're right, hon. Money is tight, but we've been scrimping on you and Andy for years. I know we have to watch it, but Ebenezer Scrooge has been around too long. He just left town."

"You mean Dad? Not fair."

"I don't mean your father, dear. I just mean the whole attitude that our family is lower on the totem pole than the doctors and lawyers, people like that. Well, we are lower, bottom line, but only in dollars. Would I trade my kids for any two in town?"

"I dunno. Had any offers?"

"Actually, yes, a few. I considered them. But – in the end ... "

"In the end, you're stuck with us."

"I guess. But the arrangement, the credit card in your name, for now, just between us. O.K.?"

"I've never really hid anything from Dad before."

"I know, hon, and that's wonderful. I just don't want to add any burden. Things haven't been going too great at work, near as I know. He doesn't open up much." Now I'm walking on thin ice, she thought. With the children, I must go slow, the time for full revelation is not now and may never come. Ease into the new affluence slowly. I can dream of palatial homes, luxury cars, trips to the seven seas, but those things must be my secret. I've shared with Galen and he is not pleased with what I'm about. The man is forty-six years old and, as they say in these parts, set in his ways. But the kids are young. I wish they could be young forever.

Meg said, "And Andy?"

"I have some special plans for that young man. He kills himself at work and school; the kid needs some relief. All in good time. I'm working on it, hon."

"Hey, that's great. I fight with him a lot but he is a wonderful guy. And he is stretched out, to the limit. Help wanted."

"Your brother is too conscientious for his own good. The kid caused us a load of grief in his early high school days when he was messing around. Your Dad and I washed those episodes out of our minds, but I know they still bother Andrew."

"Yeah, they were hairy days as I remember. Police, courts, probation officers, the whole lot. Now look at my darling bro, the man actually made a comeback."

So, unknown to Galen and Andy, the two ladies of the family, mother and daughter, close buddies, talked and laughed and planned for the future. I'm letting in a trace of sunshine, thought the mother, but not too much. Just attempting to fashion a fine line between reassurance and hiding, like the dark secret it is, the source of our money and exactly what deviousness I am into these days. Galen, I am certain, will be proud of the way I've handled the delicate balance, at least to this point. I have tough sessions ahead with my beloved husband. Can I handle that assignment as well as I've handled this one? I know he wishes I would pack it in, perhaps even has convinced himself that, with the success of the Boles' project, I will be content to take the money and run. If so, that sweet man has a rude awakening in store. Take the money, for damn sure. Run, never. Would a person go to dental school for years, pull one tooth and call it a career? Cassandra giggled; the allusion was so ridiculous. My sense of humor, even if a bit cockeyed, is still intact, a reasonable conclusion.

If I had no family, beyond Galen, this would be a slam dunk. But I have this precious boy and girl. I cannot imagine the emptiness of a life without them. They simply add a dimension that must be folded into the picture and accommodated.

Some day. We all live in a world of some day when there are no problems, no complexity. But really, in a future time when the kids are educated and on their own, I might open the door to my secret world and let them enter. If things go well in my future endeavors, there will be such a surplus of "bread" that no one in this family will ever go hungry.

My kids will triumph in their chosen fields, fortified by brains and great training and the old man and myself

60

will explore the wonders of the earth, traveling first class and dining on sirloin and lobster. So long Burger King and Wendy's. We've had a great run but your days with this tribe are numbered. White tablecloths and linen napkins suit my style, at least the style that I aspire to.

The Criminal Housewife

CHAPTER 8

Over Guinness beer, the lawyers, who occasionally liked a taste of old Erin, black and bitter though it was, moaned and groaned about the vicissitudes of life and the frustrations of the legal jungle, where only the valiant, the intelligent and the lucky survive.

"This developer, Jensen Associates it's called, but that's cover, it's really just old Steve Jenson, is gonna put me in the psyche ward before he's through." DeShales pulled at his Guinness mournfully. "Son of a bitch." He searched for words. "Son of a bitch," he repeated, too agitated to search for a simile.

"Yeah, I've heard he's rough. His way or no way."

"Double-crossed me at the Zoning. And not two hours after we'd gone over everything to be in sync. Left me swinging in the hot air. Lots of it there."

"Drop him."

"Can't."

"Money?"

"Ain't it always the case? Friggen dough, the fat bastard is twenty per cent of my gross. Mama needs new shoes, hell, new fur coat, new car, trade-in, that is. What I should do is drop her. Keep Jensen."

"Not so smooth at home?"

"Yeah. Rough water all the way. Half the time I'm afraid Shirl will walk. Half the time, I'm afraid she won't."

"I've been there. Hell of a way to live."

"Tell me about it." A long sigh. "Hey, Jimmy, couple

refills here. I must be doing penance, drinking this sludge."

"You love it. Great brew. Thick enough to eat with a spoon."

"Anyway," Zack continued. "Psycho ward is not too bad. Heavy with lawyers. Meet a lot of old friends there. Even ex-wives."

"That's a lock."

"Tell them to save a bed for me."

"Yeah. How's it going for you?"

"It ain't," muttered Zack Taylor. "Dull as dirt. Haven't had any excitement or decent payday since that blonde broad had her disagreement with Boles. And that was over two months ago." The plaintiveness was thick as an accent. "Now I'm about broke again. Not broke, but low."

"Nice piece of change though."

"Yeah, saved my year more or less. One forty for the striking Mrs. Janes. Seventy for me."

"Not bad, in fact, lovely. And no friggin Zoning Board. No egomaniac developer. No labor strikes, no material shortages. A deal, I'd say."

"Um, yeah. But I earned it. Man, the meetings, the negotiations, the threats, the bullshit."

"You handled it, buddy. Horatio at the bridge. They shall not pass. Like that."

"It's my bag. I oughta be good for something. And you remember, or do you, no paper trail, just like Cassandra wanted. With all the legal posturing, we never had to reach the point of filing a brief. Just pretend to file, promise to file. Goddamn threaten to file, but no filing." He grinned remembering. "I don't know to this day how we pulled it off but, legally, the case doesn't exist. Mr. Precedent never came to call."

"Wonderful. That was amazing. A coup they call it. Or luck, whatever."

Tom DeShales pondered the strange workings of the law. "But tell me, squire, why no paper trail? I mean to say her fixation on that aspect? Afraid the Enquirer or some such periodical would get on it?"

"Naw, I don't think so. But look at it this way. The woman has a nice old man, Galen's tops, if a little lacking in ambition. Been at that hardware store forever. And two kids, one at the "U", has his mind on our noble calling some sweet day. I'm downplaying it to Cassandra, though."

"Good. Just what we need. New blood, more competition. Unless he goes into government law. Let him joust for a cushy spot with all the other tax supported ones."

"Don't get on that, Tom. A lot of those jobs are real ball-breakers. Anyway, we're all tax supported, one way or another. You ever pay tuition to send your kids to public school? Like that."

"No wonder you get along with the blonde so well. One more socialist, no need to recruit."

"Well, socialist or friggin far right. Don't we know any people in between?"

"A vanishing breed," DeShales, beset by personal problems, sighed. "But you did say she was a wild bra burner in her college days."

"You're exaggerating. I forget some things I say. But the bra is sacred, I don't disremember such vital and intriguing information."

"Wouldn't the fair Cassandra's reluctance to leave a paper trail suggest to the objective person, if such a person exists, that in the future, no priors is a wonderful thing?"

"Could, perhaps. But you're taking a narrow view. Any of us want priors?"

"Well, you look at it that way."

"I am a true and dedicated representative at the bar. I take it seriously. What my client wants, believes, that's what I want. Isn't that the heart and soul of legal representation?"

"Thank you, professor."

The two men relaxed. Favorite watering hole, favorite

time of day. Attorneys can't make it without letting down their hair, letting the belt out a notch – semblance of peace.

"So, all this leads me to think you've been keeping track of the aforementioned blonde client."

"I've seen her three, four times. Guess I'm her family attorney now. Cozy, huh? Her and Galen."

"I had the feeling you had the procreative urge for her."

"Well, good morning." Zack Taylor grinned wickedly. "What the hell, I have that for a lot of women. There's many a slip twixt the urge and the hip. Am I quoting correctly? You're the lit man."

"Close enough. She wasn't interested?"

"Maybe, maybe not. You can't always tell with broads. Hell, you know that. But Cass is a home girl, more power to her. So sure, I'd love to nail her, but it'll most likely never happen."

"Way it goes. For every skin I've nailed to the barn door, a hundred more slipped away into the woods."

"Where, life being what it is, some other lucky stiff will nail 'em. Once or repeatedly."

"The great game. But Shirl won't let me play. I'm retired. Not undefeated. Often defeated. Yet, she goes her way. The dog in the manger bit."

"Drink up, fellow loser. We still have our health, sort of, our hair, partially, our wits, halfway."

They slugged the black stuff down and, grimacing, went for another round. That's Guinness, bracky and bitter, it gets you with the smoky past remembrances of green hills and crowded pubs.

They left the bar. Zack, back to his office for some night catch-up work, the never ending grind of chores in the "in" basket. DeShales to his elegant split level on a lovely rise looking down on much of the city. He pulled into the garage and entered through the connecting door. No dinner aroma saluted him.

The house was dark and quiet. Tom DeShales found a

note, where he expected, taped to the bathroom mirror. "Gone for the evening. If I had the brains God gave a Canadian Honker, I'd be gone for good. For sure. There's food in the fridge and, more importantly to you, beer also and hard stuff in the cabinet. You son of a bitch, you're getting to be a first class lush. Excuse me, third class."

Depression enveloped him. That lousy broad, she should talk – that note is longer than my office memos. And that air of uncertainty always there. No number to call, no address. I know her tricks, let me wonder if she is with a girl friend or some over the road cowboy from the truck stop. Screw her, we are definitely reaching the end of the road. Or at least we can see it from here.

DeShales glanced at the day's mail. His heart quickened with a letter, addressed to both parents, from his daughter, Kim, who was in her second year at a prestigious (and expensive) regional church-affiliated college. The letter brimmed with trivia about campus doings, trying out for a drama project – she had garnered a part – and news of spring football practice and the standings of the baseball and track teams. The girl admires the jocks; is that an omen or just healthy young athletic interest wondered her father. The mail also furnished bills in abundance, legal magazines, the usual deluge of his working life.

Beyond the family letter from Kim, their only child, DeShales could muster no interest or concentration. He watched, with detachment, a television story and the local news. True to Shirl's sarcasm, he found the liquor cabinet a distraction, if not a comfort. At ten thirty he went to bed. There was never a close encounter with sleep as he sought to contemplate his future and devise a practical approach. In the ensuing hours, practicality lost out.

***

The truck stop was ablaze with neon, an oasis in the outer darkness of two-fifteen A.M. Much like hospitals, an industry that never sleeps, three hundred and sixty-five days each year, because the trucks are always rolling. The restaurant served great food featuring bacon and eggs breakfast twenty-four hours every day. The truck drivers lounged over coffee while many of their buddies sacked out in the cell-like bedrooms provided.

But the whole enterprise, restaurant, gas pumps and convenience store, was not patronized by truckers only. The "Oil Derrick" was a favorite haunt for working men and women, farm folks and various segments of the traveling public. Nearly everyone in Crestburg and the surrounding area knew and liked the truck stop, a friendly home town place to hang out. This was not a favorite spot of Mr. Tom DeShales. He had only been in the restaurant a few times. Tom, a Country Club hanger on, continually skirted, both for personal reasons and professional exposure, the unseen borders between the high and the middle ground of society. I'm not a snob, he often told himself, nor yet a slob. He had been top one third of his class at William Mitchell Law, but, home town loyal, he had languished in his chosen field of real estate. Never inadequate, never brilliant, he remained a hewer of stone, trench warrior of the noble profession.

Now he sat in his car, scrunched behind the wheel, in the murky shadows at the edge of the parking lot and examined, with self contempt, why he was at this particular place at this ungodly hour of the morning. The cuckold he realized had, through history, always forced this dilemma. But cuckoldry can be a figment of the imagination as much as a state of reality. The knowing, painful conflict of a loved one lost, a former love discarded through alleged wrongs, these were as the grains of sand on a beach. Caught in the clutches of this conflict, Tom DeShales sat (crouched) in his car and in a turmoil of indecision viewed his wife's parked car and fought his own lonely battles with himself.

DeShales, in an alcoholic rage, decided several times for and against entering the restaurant. He studied his wife's two door Buick, as though asking the five year old car for advice on what to do. There was no question in his mind that a confrontation with some husky booth companion of Shirl's would result from blustering action. He knew that confrontation was a wimp word, more likely, more certain, a brawl. Tom DeShales had not been involved in a fist fight since high school; he could not imagine having a chance, no matter how fueled with the power and recklessness of righteous fury. And fury, hot and bitter, was building.

A moment of sudden sanity possessed him. He straightened up, turned the key and drove slowly back to the highway and home.

Have I dodged a bullet, literally and otherwise, and found in a moment of clarity a semblance of maturity, he wondered? Or have I, like the old movies, shown the white feather, a shameful thing, a repudiation of what manhood I was once endowed with?

There must be, he was more convinced than ever, a final accounting, a closure. I'll face the loneliness and legal messiness of divorce before I will ever put myself again in this sophomoric position. This was close, the next time could be catastrophic.

DeShales left the battle zone, where no battles had been fought, defeated only in his own mind and in his utter self-abasement.

At seven fifteen a.m. Shirl DeShales prepared breakfast at 2115 Hilltop Drive. Sausage and eggs, American fries, toast, coffee. Simple. Mrs. DeShales was a terrific cook when she was so inclined.

This morning she was inclined, to not only share a good breakfast, perhaps the last with Tom, but to come to an understanding. She felt, as did her husband, that a fork in the path loomed. One must be taken, perhaps the one less traveled.

"Three, four hours of sleep, Thomas?"

"You, maybe. I hit the sack early."

"Indeed?" Shirl had expected the games would be played, what else?

"Let's start the morning with a little truthfulness. A wonderful way to begin a new day."

"Yeah? Like where were you last night?"

She laughed. "I know perfectly well where I was. I know who I was with." Shirl buttered her toast thoughtfully. "And, of course, I know where you were around two a.m. Your Sable is easier to spot than you think. What a detective you'd make, a regular Sam Spade."

Tom DeShales felt a dull pain in his abdomen.

"You were parked in the rear area of the Oil Derrick. Exactly why, I don't know. I could hazard a guess but I would rather hear it from you. Like no more lies. Is that a possibility?"

This was a hammer blow. Tom DeShales sipped his coffee while his legal mind searched for an out. There was none.

"Shirl," he said, as evenly as he could muster, "you are, of course, correct. I was there because you were there and not at home."

"Right. And what was there for me to be at home for? I know, but you tell me."

"Why do most married women stay home?"

"For a lot of reasons, Tom. They love and admire their husbands. They're afraid of being labeled floozies, loose, horny, whatever. Or, mostly, they are scared of their husbands. None of these reasons apply to me or ever will."

"Tell me about it."

"Be patient, darling, I intend to. First, I don't love or admire you. I did once, for many years, but not now. Second, people can say what they damn please, it's a free country peopled by free men and women. I have never strayed, not yet, but I'm getting close. And third, I am not scared of my husband, or of any man. Most men are cowards, truth be told, and you well may have entered their ranks."

"You were a teacher once. Now you're teaching again. Teaching and preaching."

"I can always teach again. And very probably will if I can get recertified."

"I guess you could."

"Do you mind if I elaborate on the first point?"

DeShales snorted. Physically tired and brain fatigued though he was, he knew that this was a torrent he could not dam. "Carry on."

"The years pile up. You may not remember how it was when we began. But I do. I was so in love with you, it was breathtaking. And why not? A young, handsome, slim attorney, fresh from Bill Mitchell, Inc. or whatever it's called. You were the catch of the day and I was the luckiest young school marm in the area. Love, honor, hell, I didn't even flinch at obey like they do now. You were a young god to me, Tom, right there on the old pedestal."

"But I fell off?"

"Yeah. Well, maybe slipped more than fell. Nobody falls, I guess, it's a slow process."

"Cumulative."

"Right. Gradually you got old and sloppy. We all have to get older, the sloppy is our own choice."

"I'm not a blimp, you know."

"Of course not. But you are too fat, you eat too much, drink too much, gamble too much. Maybe even fish too much."

"You can't fish too much. And I don't lose at gambling."

"Not money. How about time, energy, misplaced priorities? You and that bunch of losers, like what's his name, Hack?"

"Actually, Zack. For Zackery."

"What I'm getting at, hon, I can still call you hon, even if you do idiotic things like midnight skulking, trying to catch your wife in some wild tryst. You were a champ, why not still a champ?"

"Lawyering is tough. Tougher than a boiled owl. Especially in the real estate end."

"Sure it is. All jobs are tough. Otherwise they wouldn't be called jobs, would they? Try welding or insurance or retail. Or a hitch in the infantry."

"Or truck driving."

"Hey, slap shot there, cowboy. Of course I know some truck drivers. Mostly nice guys, doing a brutal job the best they can."

"And lonely?"

"Ah well, I know the feeling. But I never climbed up to that sleep space behind the cab. Not for lack of invitations. Truck drivers are very hospitable."

Tom DeShales was suddenly weary of the game, the feints, the shadow boxing.

"Are we leading somewhere?"

"God, I hope so. This attrition has gone on for years."

"A truce?"

"I'm obliged, hon, you said the word, But it's hard for both of us. We dictate terms, we're dictating. Not a proper basis."

"See what you mean."

"But we have to start somewhere. Like culture, for instance. We haven't been to a play or concert in years."

"We been to the movies," the irony irresistible.

"Great. Lousy stories and salty language, about the size of it."

"OK, agreed. We'll dial up the tone."

"And here we get, as you say, preachy, which I detest. But could you agree on that great word, moderation? Less food, the fatty stuff, less drink, more exercise. Isn't that a modest request?"

"Really is. And better for my health. Agreed."

"And a little more attention to the old lady. I am your ball and chain. For now."

"Believe it or not, Shirl, I've been thinking along the

same lines. I've been remote, inattentive and what, stingy, tight, I guess. I can't buy your loyalty but I can make a down payment on it."

Shirl laughed. She felt suddenly good, as though a rickety bridge had been crossed in safety. "You aren't stingy, hon, or we wouldn't be living in this house and Kim in that fancy school. As you've often reminded me, money doesn't grow on trees. Corny old saying, can't you come up with a better one?"

"No." Tom DeShales felt better now, younger, more in charge. "But I can put some meat on those chicken bones. Your Buick is five years old, needs work. I'll look into the situation."

"Thanks, big spender, might turn out to be your wisest investment. And one thing more."

"I'm listening."

"If you had followed through last night, you'd have found me having coffee and gabbing, for hours, with Nancy Thompson. She's my best gal pal. I'd be lost without her."

"Don't know Ms. Thompson. Does she have – problems?"

"If you mean man problems, sure. Who the hell in the female gender is without them? We help each other, we are counselors without portfolio."

"Aren't we all?"

"Guess so," Shirl was pensive. "It seems, really does, that somehow, some way, we are making progress this morning. I don't want to kid myself on that score but – what do you think?"

Tom DeShales felt a great weight lifting, a removal. The recent antagonism, the wild emotions of the night before, belonged to another time, another person.

"Progress, yes. For sure. We had to make progress or regress. Status Quo never remains Quo."

"I've been tough on you, hon, even the B. word. Not all bad, you need tough love. So do I and I take my share of the blame. Not all, but my share."

"You're right about how I've let myself go. I play a little golf, riding cart of course, chase deer a couple days in hunting season and tell myself I'm keeping in shape. Shape – like a basketball." He sighed. "Exercise, what a word. But I'll learn to love the enemy." He eyed her appreciatively, for the first time in months. "You keep a figure that could knock the eyeballs off a cigar store Indian."

"Haven't tried that one – yet." She laughed like a girl, something had returned. "And, by the way, what do you know about a deal at Boles? Something about an alleged shoplifting?"

"Very little," he lied, forgetting his inward pledge to be more truthful.

"What little I know is that your old pal, Zack, is involved. Nancy was in the Boles Court when the lady, Cassandra Janes is her name, got nabbed. So Nancy was called in to the office to give what witness version she could. The deal never got to Court, so I hear."

"I'll be damned."

"Possibly. Nancy seemed to think, well, she couldn't put her finger on it, but something – "

"Yeah?"

"Something seemed very strange about the whole situation. Kind of off key, know what I mean?"

"Actually, no. But what the hell do I know about shoplifting? One bad habit I didn't master."

"You just didn't put your mind to it."

The Criminal Housewife

CHAPTER 9

If the plan gets too cumbersome, it will not work. I strive for simplicity, thought Cass, do not mess up the drill with complications, ifs, ands, buts, maybes, just keep your eye on the goal, no distractions. It is now two months since the final Boles settlement.

Get the tool, case the location, adjust the timing. Then, when the time is propitious (I love the word) just goddamn do it and never look back. She felt the freedom and exultation of a polar explorer; to go where others feared to strike for riches of not only money but the gratification of achievement.

So, ninety miles from home, Cass walked into an outdoor specialty store in Minneapolis called "The Mountaineer" and began the process. She examined knives, not the weak and ineffectual pocket variety nor the Swiss wonders of a thousand uses; these will not do. She needed something with heft and precision, but not overly large. With a salesman's help, she zeroed in.

"My hubby likes a good hunting knife. Seems like a neat anniversary present, don't you think?"

"For sure, Ma'am. Hunters love their stickers, next to their guns. Let me show you a few."

Cass examined several, then selected a beautiful midsize hunting knife in a tan scabbard. It felt balanced and right in her hand.

"How much?"

"Eighty-five. And this is top quality."

"Yes, I see." She smiled her sunniest good wife smile.

"I'll give you a hundred, even."

"Say what?"

"This baby has a nice edge, nice point. But my husband hates knife sharpening. You must have a back room, with the right tools, whetstone, like that?"

"Sure."

"Well, Bill, it is Bill isn't it?" Looking at the nice man's jacket label.

"Yeah."

"Put an edge and a point on this baby that my hubby won't have to mess with. He skins his own deer, no fetching it to the local meat cutter for Jerry. For an extra fifteen, can you do that? If you can't, the deal's off. But, that's it, one hundred or bust."

"Lady, I'll give you an edge that'd split a gnat's hair. Give me ten minutes."

And so it went at the outdoor store. Cass left with an instrument of scalpel keenness. She discarded the wrapping in a street trash can, then headed for Minneapolis International Airport, hub center for Northwest Orient. The city had outgrown old borders and was now surrounded on three sides by captive residents who complained bitterly and constantly about the danger and noise of low flying behemoths that shook their homes on take-offs and landings. The fourth side presented a frog lover's paradise in the marshes of the Minnesota River, two miles before its confluence with the Mississippi.

Cass did not know the airport too well; flights with Galen had been few and far between, and the astounding terminal was constantly being renovated and enlarged.

After parking, Cass sauntered through the passenger terminal, thronged as always with hundreds of people. True to the drill, she did not hurry; she had all the time in the world. A gallows humor brought a smile to her face. No hurry, baby, the gals in the women's slammer at Shakopee have plenty of time, also. You dumb losers, junkies, killers, child abusers – slave to some burglary and bag man boyfriend who got you in deep shit, then vanished. I love good men, mused Cass, the bad ones need a taste of my new knife, in some romantic area.

The hum of human noise was all about. Barely audibly, she threw her challenge to whatever gods decide the fate of law breakers. "You poor misguided broads, this is one gal that's a mile ahead of you. Because I'm smart and I don't have an ass for a husband." Cass was nearly euphoric, a sudden high she did not discourage. Now, to herself, I need this feeling of utter confidence. I've got it and I'll never lose it till hell freezes over because I am Cassandra Janes, and I can handle anything!

She sashayed through the commercial area, stopping for a sandwich and a Coke. The drive from Crestburg had sharpened her appetite. She considered, only for a moment, a refreshing cocktail but told herself, this is a test, forget it.

Cass entered one of the many concourses. She worried about the knife at the security check, but her bag sailed through without comment or sounding of alarms. She picked up her bag and continued down the concourse. No one at this stage ever asks for a ticket or a boarding pass, the airport administration unknowing or uncaring if she was intending to board a flight or was meeting friends or relatives arriving.

Cass wandered the concourse, then crossed over on a connecting ramp to another concourse. She didn't know exactly what she was looking for but rode a keen instinct that she would recognize the best location on sight. And it was imperative to concentrate on whatever concourse that stationed A.M. flights to the Windy City.

Very few of the moving sidewalk people movers had been installed by 1995, many more would follow. Travelers chugged their way on foot from one flight station to another or, if lame or elderly, rode the electric carts that constantly threaded their way through teeming crowds. Cass studied the various maps to know more precisely, though she doubted she would need the knowledge, the entire network of concourses and their connecting corridors.

The bustling areas all seemed much the same. Carpets covered all floors, easy on the feet, yet very firm. She touched the surface in a couple of places and discovered, as she had remembered, a kind of plastic sheen on the surface, an alligator skin, she thought, to handle the tremendous traffic and preserve the carpet body.

In no hurry, she watched and carefully observed, as she strolled.

Then, the time was right, the ebb and flow thick and vital around her. She dropped to one knee (hey, I know this maneuver by now). With her bulky coat covering her action, she grasped the knife and plunged it into the floor. Her action satisfied her apprehension, the razor sharp instrument cut through the carpet like a table knife through butter.

She slipped the hunting knife back in her bag, finished with her shoe strap, rose and continued her leisurely ramble.

One tiny step. She had been determined to know for certain. Now she knew, with a certainty, that the master plan was operable. If the knife had been blunted by the carpet surface, all bets were off, at least for this particular mode of operation.

Cass was fascinated by the human panorama encountered in the concourses and the commercial center, the teeming, hurrying folks, some calm with the long, boring experience of travel. Some were stressed and nervous, faces taut with the tension of unfamiliarity. Brisk businessmen and women, young couples with straggling children, even babies, and the rainbow of dress and origin. She marveled at swarthy men with turbaned heads, cloistered women with dark clothing and tiny slits for the eyes – how can they see?

And where are they going? Strange residents of nations unfriendly to ours, yet free as birds to come and go as they pleased. Orientals, also, in sparse numbers, but favoring suits and ties in contrast to the casual attire of many Midwesterners.

Young people always drew her attention, her own two always on her mind. Most were beautiful young animals, full of laughter and nonchalance. Others, a few, repulsed her. She could hack the earrings of the young men, that had been an easy accommodation over the years. But the nose rings, lip rings and, aglitter in the crowd, one young lady whose smile displayed the metal of a pierced tongue. Good Lord, thought Cass, I'm still, with all my failings, spiritual enough to embrace the notion that the body is the dwelling place of the soul and you do not desecrate your body, the beautiful body that was given to you.

Hang on, am I approaching hypocrisy here? Am I playing mind games I'm doomed to lose? I contemplate a kind of desecration, a punishment, of my own body while putting down another way. Forget it, Cass, and concentrate on the handsome men and women, the beautiful older folks, the bustle of humanity's migrating instincts. Much safer.

Back to the parking ramp. Home to Crestburg, to home and family, comfort and safety. I live two lives, she thought, housewife and scam artist. And, no dishonor to my precious husband, the second is becoming more exciting than the first. Excitement is, truly, a narcotic and I'm becoming more and more addicted. I've got to watch that carefully.

And carefully she guarded her inner feelings on the ninety miles to Crestburg, past small towns and picture-book farms. With all the dangers and uncertainties facing her in the weeks ahead, this remarkable woman drove the busy four-lane in peace, the trauma filed away.

Cassandra had never lost her love for the scenic

beauty of her home state. Not a true hunter and gatherer like Galen, she had little interest in hunting and fishing. She was a bird watcher, a worshiper of the autumn panorama of changing colors. Southeast Minnesota is farm country but the swatches, mostly on hillsides, of oak and maple and hickory, staples of pioneer barn raising, and the soft woods of poplar and willow reached full majesty at different times, prolonging the fall season for many weeks. There are canvasses of pure beauty here beyond, perhaps, what other nations, other continents could offer. So I believe, but I am not positive, and, in wondrous uncertainty, I will check out those areas when my time arrives.

She swerved slightly while gazing. Watch the damn driving, she scolded, or else park and get out. No slips allowed, my schedule is too exact. This old bucket of bolts has served us well but, my lord, a one car family in this day and age. But fancy new wheels are in the future and there will be a car for each of us, top drawer, you can bet your boobies on that.

Entering Crestburg, she headed for home, then changed directions and drove to the Cherokee Shopping Center. Scene of the crime, she thought, as she parked the car and walked into Boles Department Store.

Why not, indeed? My problems with Boles are all in the past. They've been good to me, look at it that way. Why shouldn't I throw some business their way? I had almost forgotten, thinking about the knife, that another piece of merchandise was just as important. I simply do not own the proper kind of shoes for this project. She sauntered past the purse display on her way to the shoe department.

Cassandra spent fully three fourths of an hour surrounded by footwear. Her feet were large, eight and one-half, and finding the right size and style was time consuming. The patient clerk trotted out pair after pair before she was satisfied. She bought a pair of shiny black leather pumps, with just the right heel. Not excessively high or spiky, but extremely stylish, with a small heel print, one hundred and twenty dollars.

"My, I'm certainly peeling out those C notes today," she murmured. "But I've got them and Boles needs the money, they've had rough luck lately."

Now, I've got to go into training on these beauties, she thought. All my life I've walked around on ordinary shoes, never went in for glass slippers for the grand ball. My feet need some serious readjustment. I'll wear these babies around the house when I'm alone, maybe even go on short hikes. These costly gems have got to become second nature to me if I'm going to operate in Minneapolis.

***

"Mom," said Andy, "I know Dad's been talking to you about my ... troubles." In the living room of the old home, Andy, for the first time in years, felt awkward, out of sync with the world and his mother.

Cassandra relished any moments with her son, gone most of the year from home. A long history of growing-up problems lay behind them. The son had emerged from the ashes of teen addiction to become a virtual poster child of the power and persuasiveness of tough love and rehab, the turning around that is always wished for, so seldom attained. She said, "What trouble? I thought you were a tough guy."

Andy laughed, he knew his mother too well.

"I'm tough, Mom. I'm smart, I apply myself, and I'm certainly going to end up with lousy grades, even flunk out." He sighed. "Made it through this year, skin of my teeth. No chance next year on my schedule."

"Your Dad and I have gone over this many times, honey. And always the same conclusion."

"Like?"

"You work too hard. Too damn hard, brutal hours for a kid taking a full load. It's going to stop."

"Oh, sure."

"Don't smart ass me, hon. Your future is our future. Next semester you're down to twelve hours a week. Your boss doesn't like it, he can stuff it. Either that or a new job entirely. Or better, no job."

"Not possible, Morn. It can't add up. We've been over this a million times. The costs are fixed in concrete."

"I'm sure."

"And not just me, Mom. I'm nothing special. Great guys and gals drop out like flies. You know the grad percentages. For a great institution, they're not good. And the jocks, even worse."

"Well, you were OK at sports but not the U Jock level. I should have fed you more Wheaties."

"And half those guys don't appreciate the sugar deal they've got."

"What they're got, mostly, is broken legs and damaged hips."

"At times, true." Andy was restive. Conversations about money in a lower middle family can be the pits. Nor did he want to broach, once again, his bail-out strategy of a four year Army hitch, served godknowswhere, to guarantee a future graduation.

Cassandra Janes looked her son squarely in the eyes and, without emotion, dropped the bomb.

"How much in your checking account, Andy?"

"Don't embarrass me."

"Hey, kid, just answer the question."

"As of... ?"

"I dunno. Couple days ago. About one forty?"

Cassandra laughed. She had not felt so good, so alive, in ages. This was the beginning of fulfillment.

"Well, look again." She handed him a bank deposit slip, dated the day previous. "Can you hack it for the next two years on this?"

And whistled. "Judas – what is this? My God, three thousand dollars!"

"You need rest and bifocals, too!" Cassandra was in a

mood, "Try again."

Then it dawned. Andy Janes, overworked, thin as a rail, looking forward glumly to a service hitch to refuel the money tank, saw redemption. "Thirty thousand, a three and a bunch of zeroes." His brain whirled in the moment of new horizons.

"Mom, you wouldn't play a joke on me like this? But it has to be some kind of a goofy prank."

Andy was floundering.

"It's real, legit, baby. Took care of it yesterday."

"But – a million questions. How, what, where – am I in journalism now?"

"I've been saving up."

"You've saved thirty big ones, from those creams and potions? Come on."

"I won a lottery."

"Nice try, Mom."

Cass tired of the gamesmanship. But Galen had to remain the only one for sharing her hidden life. Trust no one; the motto had to include her son and daughter. The discipline, the chance of a slip.

"Look, we need to have a pact on this. No questions, no answers. And Kid, please know I love you and trust you. You can see, no doling this out in pittances, time to time. That would be an insult, you're a grown-up man. You get yourself that sheep hide in the next two years. Come grad school, we'll reevaluate."

Andy stared. He could not fathom what was happening.

She said, "Agreed?"

"Yeah, of course. But..."

"Andy, I just laid out the program. No buts, no bullshit. I won't say it again."

A long pause. Like his father, who could hardly recognize his wife, Andy was confronted with a mother he had never known.

"Mom, you've got to be the most wonderful person on earth. There's some mystery here, something way beyond me."

Now Cassandra grinned. "Deal with it."

Andy smiled that sunny grin that had always gladdened his parents' heart and launched more than one lady in pursuit of this handsome young man. His mother knew in an instant, although there had been no doubts, that this slice of the Boles' generosity had been well deployed. Give the kid all the rope in the world, he will never hang himself, perhaps even invest the bulk of the money in ways more profitable than any that either parent could have devised. He's that brilliant, the thought of a doting mother; if I didn't think so, how could I be so certain he will make a great lawyer?

But that, for the time being, was considering only one offspring. Andy might have read her thoughts.

"I'll have to tell Meg. How can I luck into such a stash and not her? I can't have her jealous of me, that would kill me."

"Don't be so damn dramatic. It wouldn't kill you. And you can forget that word 'jealous.' It's not in Meg's vocabulary. And, of course, I have plans for your sister."

"Plans? Of this magnitude?"

"In time, honey, in time. Margaret is only tenth grade, for heaven's sake. We'll take care of her, in style, when the time comes. And without the two years of penance that you've put in."

"But how – never mind."

Cassandra, unperturbed, went on. "In the meantime, Meg will do as she pleases. You know what I'm talking about. It's a trial. In the past year, her 'commitment,' is that the word, has become a bit overwhelming."

"For sure, strenuous."

"Comes home every Saturday night, and some week nights, splotched with paint, hands raw, tired as a dog. Not to mention many full days with school out."

"Does Habitat for Humanity have to be that demanding?"

"I don't believe they are. Meg just makes the demands

on herself. Dedication, my lord, she's redefined the word."

"Still talking about our old ex prez, Jimmy Carter, the man who builds houses in Haiti?"

"Her hero. Other gals her age have rock stars, actors, athletes. Meg has smiling Jimmy, the peanut farmer."

Andy was troubled. "She could do a lot worse. But she has to have a break now and then, some life outside of school and putting up sheetrock. My kid sister, the carpenter, painter, plumber, what a gal! Does she do roofing?"

"Oh, hell. One of her specialties."

"That skinny little kid?"

"Not so little anymore. Or skinny for that matter. A young woman with a big heart for the halt, the lame and the blind. What chapter and verse is that? And also for the homeless." She touched Andy's arm. "I'm so glad that you're concerned, hon. You've been away so much, afraid you two were growing apart."

"Never."

"And don't worry about her financially. I'd be drawn and quartered before I'd show preferences for one of my babies over the other - trust me."

"All my life, Mom."

A few minutes later, Meg buzzed in. She kissed her mother and took a playful swipe at Andy. At fifteen, she was certainly no skinny kid, her tanned face was glowing.

"What's up, professor?"

"We've been wasting our time," said Andy, "talking about you."

"I could feel it down the street. And Mom, I'm not pregnant."

"I'm so relieved. Thing is," said Cass, "your Dad and I have figured out a way to help Andy the next two years. Keep him out of an early burnout at the big U."

"Good idea, Mom. But how so?"

"Well we – brace yourself, Carpenter, we advanced

him thirty thousand to get him off the chain-gang at the factory, back to the classroom."

"What happened - you rob a bank?"

The offhand banter struck close to home. Time again for the actress, thought Cassandra.

"I told Andy I won the lottery. I sure as hell have two nosy brats. It's really none of your business but we have saved and scrimped the best we can. That and a couple of very lucky stocks that split and went through the roof."

"Whatever. This hunk has been working too hard. I've been worried. What's it been, thirty-five hours a week and carrying a full load?"

"You should talk," said Andy. How many of those shacks you put up this year?"

"Helped on four or five. And they're not shacks. They are two bedroom, no frills houses. And the proud new owners have to pitch in with sweat equity or they're down the road, Joe."

"Discipline, huh?"

"Well, it's a beautiful program."

"Beautiful, with child labor. How come they're employing a kid your age?"

"In the first place, barrister, I'm not a kid. And I'm not an employee, just a volunteer. Don't get paid an Indian penny."

"I thought you were head contractor by now. Jill of all trades, a woman for all seasons."

"Don't be a dummy, Andy. I'm nothing more than a gofer. Carrying stuff, mixing paint, making myself useful. You oughta try it. You know what we're doing but I'll explain it again, very carefully, for the learning impaired. We're helping people who are like sardines, six to a family in a one bedroom apartment, two bedrooms at most, at Shylock rates that cut into the grocery money."

"Or beer money."

"Andy, let up. This program is head and shoulders

above all the other low-cost housing agendas. Most of the others are just subsidized rental deals. Habitat for Humanity believes in the old pioneer spirit. Homesteading. You dig the difference, big shot?"

"Sure, Meg, of course I do." Andy was tender, he adored his lovely kid sister, the one who had always stood by him in troubled times. "And Mom says she has the dough to help you when the time comes for college."

"I'll speak for myself, young man." Cassandra smiled. "But he's got it right. We are a little better off than we were."

"Great," Meg was nonchalant. "And exactly which bank was it?"

The Criminal Housewife

CHAPTER 10

Like a military operation, Cassandra spoke to her inner self, the mind that she increasingly regimented to respond correctly. Galen often, sardonically, still used the time segments that began with the letter O. Now it is 0700. I will arrive at the airport before 0900, recon and patrol and observe the area at my leisure, no set agenda. Everything depends, as Gale would say, on the terrain and the disposition of the opposing forces. There is no enemy, in actual fact. There is a deployment of unfriendlies, those who would do their best to prevent successful completion of my mission.

It's really fun to think in these terms, those used by Gale and his buddies in Nam. Those years that now seem a lifetime removed. Gale endured the evils of jungle warfare, fought the enemy, buried his friends and suffered, for years, the flashbacks and horrors of a witless war against people we did not know or hate. Then, dismissal from the service, a twelve hundred dollar state bonus, and goodbye forever. Cassandra overlooked G.I. educational benefits, granted but unused by a man who only desired the peace and tranquility of nine to five and a lot of fishing and bird hunting on the weekends.

They still owe Gale, the government, not the airport, and I am the collector; I collect when and where I can. And I have the ability, the genius, actually, to pull it off. My confidence could not be running higher – it's off the charts.

The night before had been a problem. Galen, knowing that something was coming down, but without a clue, had been curiously withdrawn. In an operation beyond his depth, beyond his concept of the marriage contract, he was yet bound by an agreed upon hands off.

"This cousin in Chicago. Not sure you've even mentioned her to me. Real or make believe?"

"Gale, she's as real as barn paint and just as colorful. Emmy and I go back to kindergarten, first, second grade. Then her folks moved away. Job transfer for her Dad."

"So. Eight years old to forty-four. Hell of a span."

Cassandra laughed. "Hardly. I visited her more than once when I was at good old UW, Madison. And we've had a few cards and letters through the years."

"Yeah, I do vaguely recall the connection. Anyway, not really bosom buddies."

"You know me, Gale. I don't have bosom buddies among women. Scads of acquaintances, damn few friends. A weakness of mine." She knew she was sparring, making up words, an exercise to cloak a fantasy trip. But the answers must be in place, answers to future questions she could not foresee. And Gale must be protected.

"Maybe I can renew friendship with an old pal, a coz I have neglected all these years." Cassandra sighed. "And, maybe not, who knows what passing time's done. We may have nothing in common."

"Well, you could use a change. If only for a week. We – you can sure as hell afford it."

"And four hundred miles, for cripes sake, my lord, people commute half that distance to work, or so I've heard."

"An early flight, you'll be in good old Chi by noon."

"Yep. I like the schedule."

"Have a good time, baby. I'll miss you."

A quick hug and kiss. "Hey, I'll miss you every minute, hon. Almost wish I wasn't going. But a girl has to get out of the house now and then."

She parked the car in the huge ramp. Then she ran a double check on her gear. The hunting knife, in its scabbard, her ticket. I haven't been in Chicago for years.

And no intention of going there this time. But the paper work must be in place. Two hundred bucks in the purse, no one heads out of town without some cash. Would look a little fishy.

Next she checked her shoes. She had worn the new slip-ons for days around the house to get accustomed to them. It had taken some time, most of her life had been spent in plain flats and low-heeled dress shoes. Plus the athletic shoes of her playground and beach days. Now the new shoes, sleek and elegant with narrow high heels, not quite stiletto but near, had required a break-in period for comfort and stability. The handsome shoes fit well and she had rehearsed the art of the quick exit, a key element in her design.

Cass entered the airport terminal building just as she had one week before. One bag to check, she wanted no carry-ons in addition to her handbag. The check line was modest, she completed the task in ten minutes, then headed for the designated concourse. Through the shopping area, she picked up a Reader's Digest and a candy bar. Then through the detectors, no problem. She checked the time, fifty minutes before the flight. Perfect for discipline, I can't goof around, but not too much time, it would look strange. What was this woman doing, nearing her flight station with hours to spare?

Questions, answers. She could never have all the answers but, at least, some of them.

She picked a concourse spot that had seemed about right on her recon mission. This was a guessing game, she thought, perhaps one piece of carpeting as good as the next. She loosened the knife in the scabbard, dropped to one knee, the bulky coat covering her action, and plunged the razor sharp blade downward. One quick stroke, then a cutting motion of a few inches. I think I've got it right but, in any case, it will have to do. The heel, I am sure, will stick nicely if my timing is correct.

And remember the iron exactitude of the drill. The drill is everything. I have set up this operation, the culmination of my hopes and dreams, for today. If the timing is off, even by a second, if the operation screams to me that I have miscalculated or the cart does not appear as I have envisioned, don't get panicky. Abandon ship, proceed with your flight to Chicago. Only you will know, and prepare for another time. This deal will work, sometime; it is not imperative that it culminates this day unless all systems are go. I am driven by ambition; I will not be driven by desperation.

But all seemed well to the moment, the blueprint unblemished in the bustling surroundings of folks coming and going, destinations both home and away.

Cassandra strolled back toward the terminal center, took the first crosswalk to the right and followed that to one of the neighboring concourses. She meandered along for several hundred feet, then decided, hey, far enough. Surreptitiously, she grasped the hunting knife, with a gloved hand, and unobserved, ditched it in one of the waste receptacles, pushing it well down into the debris. Next, she sought a women's rest room and, after washing and drying her hands, redonned the gloves and pushed the scabbard deep into the waste towel containers.

So simple, so easy. Weapons dispatched, wiped clean, far from the scene of the action.

But the action was yet to occur. Now, Cassandra sauntered back to the original concourse. She willed a kind of relaxation, split-second timing could never result from mind and muscles locked in tension. She murmured the mantra, "easy baby, easy, easy," this is a gut check and I've got the intestines.

A passenger-moving cart was approaching, weaving almost silently, expertly, through the crowded concourse. Cassandra was near the spot of the carpet slit, nearly invisible to the untrained eye.

The cart was closer now. Fifty, then forty feet. Cassandra slowed, one pace from the damaged carpet. Fifteen feet.

Her left heel jammed into the carpet slash. A cry of terror, involuntary, escaped her lips as she was thrown – as she threw herself – directly in the path of the personnel cart. Much too late, the action was so swift, the driver slammed the brake and wrenched the wheel, reflex actions to avoid the unavoidable. There was a sickening sound of hard plastic against human flesh. Cassandra's forehead crashed the plastic front and a shriek of pain escaped her as her left arm was crushed beneath the right front tire.

For a moment, silence. Then a circus atmosphere followed the accident. There were no screams, but the giant sounds of humanity, sorrow, concern, amazement filled the corridor. The driver, a retired postal clerk, was near to fainting. The passengers, older folks, were tremendously concerned, almost as though they had been at fault. Gentle hands attempted to help the fallen victim, even as the usual cautions about not moving a wounded person until medical help had arrived, were voiced. Then one of the passengers, in what seemed a rather inhumane complaint, but was only sensible, began to ask, "how will we get to our flight on time? Will they hold the plane?"

In agonizing pain, Cassandra's spirit could not be destroyed. "Hold the goddamn plane or send it off. Who gives a damn? I could use a little help here!" She was near to babbling, the indignities of hysteria closing in on her programmed brain ... the trauma at war with her iron discipline.

In her pain, she chanced a quiet glance to the side. The black pump, stylish and shiny though it was, looked forlorn, the heel still stuck into the carpet floor.

Hey, boys and girls, what have we here, the thought flashed. That fancy shoe might just be the catalyst for all of Cassandra's dreams of a wonderful future.

The Criminal Housewife

CHAPTER 11

The autumn morning in Minneapolis was still dark at six-fifteen but a beautiful day seemed at hand. No rain, a fresh breeze, the promise of sunshine, as the city came slowly to life.

There was a subdued murmur of sound from the street, a whisper that would change to a vibrant hum with the traffic of cars, trucks, police sirens and ambulances, although the sirens had been sporadic all night. Vehicles were already inching into the nearby parking ramps, the hospital located in the heart of the city, two hefty stone throws from the Metrodome. One industry was alive and stirring, the business that knows no sleep, just different shifts, the industry of the ill, the infirm, the damaged, the distraught.

Cassandra Janes lay in her narrow bed and contemplated, with irony, her uncertain future. Oh God, how I ache, she thought. And ache I should. In all my preparations, I constantly sought to guard against events going wrong. I forgot about things going too well. I fully considered a few bumps and bruises, not this cartoon black eye from the huge welt on my cheek and forehead, not the busted arm that hurts like a bastard.

I should look with distaste at the cast they have swathed my arm in, from wrist to elbow. I must remember to have Gale and the kids autograph it. But pain and discomfort aside, I look at that hard plaster with fondness. It may well become the star witness, the crowning jewel in the arsenal of Mr. Zack Taylor.

But I'm getting out of here. I can suffer as well in Crestburg as here. One night is long enough in this dungeon. I can have my own doctor at the clinic take over at home. What time is it? Six thirty. I didn't sleep all that badly; they must have slugged the drugs into me pretty good.

Galen will be here soon, the old darling. When he arrived yesterday afternoon, he wanted to stay with me, spend the night in this room, but they wouldn't let him. I'm hungry for breakfast; hope they have some decent grub.

So ran the thoughts of Cassandra in the A.M. following her traumatic experience at the airport. She had received first aid at the terminal medic center, in a room crowded with the suits and ties of harried officials, the cart driver, nurses and others Cass could not make out through the mask of pain that clouded her vision and danced the stick figures before her. The ambulance ride to General Hospital had followed and the reunion with a distraught husband who could barely conceal his anguish at the sight of the battered woman he had adored all his life. She remembered, vaguely, that Zack Taylor had surfaced, she must have called him. But two hours after her transfer to the hospital, there he was.

In less than a day, actually still only twenty hours, my life, for better or worse, has been forever altered. Not through blind accident nor some strange alignment of the planets, no unforeseen forces, but through my own deliberate action. And that's the way it should be. I'll drive this wagon right to the canyon's edge. My star is in ascendance, as near as I can determine, from this lovely private room.

Have the wheels been set in motion, is "justice" grinding along its glacial path, she wondered. I have to stay cool, not sweat the details for a few days. Zack can handle things, he's been tested by Boles. I'll be OK if I stay the painful course. I'm tough, tougher than roofing nails. I'll be OK. Except – except not too OK, not on the surface. My goal must be to conduct a clinic on suffering. With this swollen face and busted wing, that shouldn't be too difficult. Cass smiled, she felt almost cheerful as a hearty breakfast was placed on her tray and her bed raised up to a comfortable sitting position. With one hand, she tried to feed herself. The action was awkward, strained, a lesson in partial disability.

The great game. The fantastic fulfillment of my life, what I have dreamed of and planned for all these years is at hand. As they say at the Olympics . . . Let the Games Begin!

She looked up as two familiar figures appeared beside her bed. Both Galen and Andy had arrived the day before, the call must have been made from information on her I.D. Cassandra had no recollection, as with Taylor, of having called them. Dear to her heart as they were, part of her wished they had not come, the danger of the personal overshadowing the mission.

She could barely recall her husband and son from the day before. Had they arrived in the afternoon or evening? Before or following Taylor? Cassandra was not certain and the timing was irrelevant to the game. She hugged them both and even managed some tears, real as life, from her eyes, one of which was a swollen purple.

"Looking good, Mom," said Andy, his cracked voice not equal to the banter.

"You crazy, wonderful darling." Galen was nearly overcome. "Yesterday I nearly died. Today I feel reborn."

"Hell, Gale, you don't look any the worse for wear. But thanks, hon."

"I'm so damn happy that you're still with us. And better here than Chicago."

"Oh, God." Cass was contrite. "I forgot, just floated out of my mind. Call Emmy."

"I did that yesterday, doll. Remember, you left the name and telephone number on the fridge."

"What a relief! Thanks hon. It just now flashed through me, Emmy waiting for me to show up at her place. Lucky we didn't plan for her to meet me at O'Hare."

"Mom, are you really OK?" Andy was so stricken that Cassandra felt, for the first time, a stab of conscience. "How long will you be here?"

She groaned. "Ah, there's some pain. And this cast will take some getting used to."

"For sure, Mom. But this is a great hospital, they'll take good care of you."

"I know, honey. But I'd rather heal at home. I'm out of here today if your Dad will agree. He'll have to drive me to Crestburg. Gale, darling, you're missing work. And, Andy, get back to school."

Galen grinned. "You're giving a lot of orders for a woman flat on her backside. We'll see what the doctor says."

The tension had evaporated, the family, minus Meg, laughed and joked, a strange parody at this juncture in their lives, with only Mom aware of the true implications. Poor Meg, down with a sore throat, had been prevented by her Dad from making the trip to Minneapolis.

A few minutes later Zack Taylor walked in. He had stayed over at the Hilton and was brisk and businesslike in attitude, the true professional. He shook hands with Andy and Galen, then requested, with great politeness, a few minutes alone with his client.

The few minutes turned out to be over half an hour while the husband and son cooled their heels in the waiting room. Galen was so shaken and perplexed he could not think coherently. To have his wife go off on some strange adventure he barely understood was one thing, but extreme physical danger, brutal, life-threatening, was another. Accident, preprogrammed inevitability? Galen Janes had in a sense been alerted beforehand. The intelligence was there; he had not picked up on the possibilities. He wondered, had Cass herself weighed all the costs?

Andy, with no preliminary knowledge, grasped intuitively that strange events were coming down. The reality, the incisiveness of pre-law clawed at his brain. None of this was mentioned to his father as they waited. Galen, eyes heavy-lidded, lit one cigarette from the butt of another, a silent defiance to the "no smoking" sign on the wall.

Zack Taylor, the rock the Janes family clung to, emerged from the patient's room. His visit with Cassandra had gone well and, while waves of pain twisted the bruised face occasionally, she had been able to convey forcefully to the attorney her anger... more than anger... deep fury at the indignities that had been visited on her. The fire in her eyes, one nearly closed, blazed. They had discussed in detail what had occurred and Cassandra's last words, not unexpected, were "Get those sons of bitches, Zack. They can't do this to Cass Janes and walk away."

"Here's what we've got to do, Galen," said Zack. "Your wife has had a terrible thing happen to her, a near-tragedy really. An accident, sure, but avoidable by any accepted standards of commercial precaution."

"God, Mr. Taylor, my Mom could have been killed"

"Exactly, Andy."

"So – what now?" Andy was as lost as his father.

"Well, now, first things first. Galen, your wife has a round-trip ticket to Chicago, not used. I could try to get it cashed in but it is better if a family member does." He sighed. "Takes time I believe. They won't hand over the cash, but get the process rolling."

He paused, pawing through his briefcase for other matters he had noted. "You guys came here together, I take it? No, that can't be right, you're over at the "U" Andy?"

"Yeah"

"Well, we are three people, four cars. Some one has to rescue Mrs. Janes' car from the ramp. She gave me the parking ticket. You know how those charges mount.

Before long they're more than the car is worth."

"Easy," said Galen. "I'll follow Andy over to his place, then we'll come back here together. I'll get Cass' car and turn in my rental car."

"Fine. And in a couple days or more, whenever your wife can be moved, come back for her. Either that or she can take the limo home. By that time she won't need an ambulance. You have one tough wife there, Galen."

"Tough or awkward, Zack."

"Don't be too hard on the little lady. Accidents happen. Why they're called accidents, I suppose. I've even seen you go ass over appetite on the squash court."

"Still get to my feet to handle you, buddy."

"In your dreams."

For the first time in two days, Galen grinned. He felt near to buoyant, someone was looking out for them, someone had the situation in hand.

He grasped the attorney's right hand.

"Thanks. I appreciate all you've done, Zack. And all you're going to do." Galen saw a road ahead, one he did not wish to travel. The smart ass attorney would travel that road with Cass, to what destination he would not guess.

And so, in one of the somber waiting rooms of General Hospital, Minneapolis, legal ripples were set in motion, waves that would culminate in the weeks and months ahead into a game of bluff and counter bluff, more meaningful than any of the midnight poker games of Taylor, DeShales and other assorted low rollers in the lovely city of Crestburg.

The Criminal Housewife

CHAPTER 12

The autumn weather had been, as is common in the Midwest, streaky. A few days of good harvesting weather, interspersed with periods of cold rain and blustery winds. October's bright blue weather, said the poet. Not always.

But cold outside contributes to warmth within. Within walls, within the belly. Zack Taylor and Tom DeShales had deserted their favorite watering hole for the down home cooking and cold beer of the Alpine restaurant. A long, leisurely lunch, what the hell, we travel this way once, often convinced that once was more than sufficient. Banana crème pie for Tom, pecan pie for Zack. Comfort foods for the already well upholstered added to the contentment quotient.

"Jensen finally came around, fuming and fighting and cussing all the way. The man hates to give in on anything, don't matter how trivial."

"So, it's all systems go on the fabulous North by Northwest development?"

"I, cross my battered fingers, hope so. We're a hell of a lot closer than we were two months ago."

"Those three hundred grand homes ought to throw a red road block at the affordable housing situation."

"Don't sneer, barrister. That's a whole different story and I appreciate the problem more than most folks. Hell, I live and breathe real estate."

"Sounds like the set speech for the rich apologist."

"Zack, Zack. The little Caesars that buy these homes will buy from Jensen or someone else, that feature upscale homes. Or they'll go live somewhere else, farther out in the country. Or Austin, that new pig sticking plant don't smell like the old one. And other towns welcome the moneyed class, just like we do."

"I welcome the knowledge."

"I conduct easy seminars."

Zack Taylor drank his beer. Not the correct move for early afternoon. He said, "Personal questions are taboo in some cultures."

"Fortunately, we're not cultured."

"Right. So what's with the home front?"

DeShales did not resent the query. Too many years of banter and concern lay between them. "Aw, hell, Zack, I ain't got the guts of a spaded cat. I gave in, crawled you might say."

"Yeah."

"Begged her to stay. I'll shape up, all that corn. And, amazing grace, she agreed that our troubles were part her fault. A small part, granted."

"Hey, Tom, great. Progress, huh?"

"You might say," Tom grinned. "But was it for me, or that new BMW I sprang for?"

Zack whistled.

"New BM – Wow! For a new BM, even a Lexus, you can sleep with me."

"Now you tell me."

They finished the desserts, then ordered a second round of beers. Samuel Adams, draft, this time, with a foamy collar and mahogany hue.

"I've been saving the best for the last. On my activities, I am duty bound to issue you a full report," said Zack.

"I'd hope so or disciplinary action could follow."

"Got a new case. A block buster, an Apollo shot. Biggest case of my undistinguished career. Personal injury to end all P.I. deals."

"Car wreck?"

"No. Well, sort of. You're a traveling man, Tom. At airports you know those little cars, tad bigger than a golf cart, that chug around the concourses, carrying old or disabled passengers to the correct station."

"Yeah, often been tempted to ask for a lift. Never did, couldn't stand the sarcasm which would certainly be forthcoming. Big gut remarks."

"Right." Zack drew a deep breath, savoring the moment. "Well, this gal, this lady, was sashaying down the corridor to catch her flight to Chicago. Caught her heel on a tear in the carpet. Tossed her, tit over teakettle, right under the wheels of the convenience cart."

"My Lord," DeShales whistled. "And this was where, at Minneapolis? Bastion of Northwest."

"Yeah. Guess I didn't mention that. We don't have those carts at the local strip."

"She get hurt, bad?"

"You might say. Bruises on the face, leg scratches. And the golden egg, catch of the day, a broken arm."

"When did all this happen?"

"Few days back. I've been swamped with the case and her family."

"But – Minneapolis?" DeShales was stunned.

"How in hell did you get involved. Your network's bigger than I imagined?"

Zack grinned, a wicked smile that split his face. This, with his old friend, was pure enjoyment.

"It was a local lady."

"No kidding. Anyone I know?"

"Well, sort of. You know of her. My old client from earlier in the year, Cassandra Janes."

DeShales was incredulous. He gasped for words but no words formed. Then he chuckled, increasing the volume to a huge laugh, one that startled the customers. He wiped his eyes to regain control.

"This is fantasy."

"Good word. Suits me."

"She, Mrs. Janes, gets bowled over in the Minneapolis International Airport, then calls you, for old times sake."

"Sort of. More to it than that crude assessment. I

prefer to think she contacted me for legal counsel of a kind tried and tested before." Another satanic grin. "Go for the best."

"Right. Yeah, right. Damnedest thing I ever heard of. Amazing."

"We live in an amazing age."

"Same woman, good looker, as I remember you describing her. Blonde, yeah, blonde, at least then."

"And still."

"How do you account for all this?"

"All what?"

"Within a few months. Same person, different problem. But difficulties for you, buddy, to handle."

"You won't believe my theory."

"Try me. Please try me, I'm floundering."

"The long arm of coincidence."

A long silence. Then from DeShales, "Hm. Can the long, long arm possibly reach that far?"

"Guess it can. Guess it has."

DeShales pondered. Experienced lawyer, this was beyond his depth. And, he recalled, a few months previously, they had come near to arguing on the misadventure or bad luck of Cassandra Janes.

"Well," he murmured carefully, "who the hell is to judge that in a cockeyed world strange and wondrous things may occur."

"I've never had a case this big. Should say, potentially this big. And, as before, deep pockets."

"And, as before, half the alumni of Harvard Law in the opposite trenches."

"Can't touch us," a hint of bravado, "we are teflon coated on this baby. We are way beyond the legal pyrotechnics of those who are dedicated to the protection and enhancement of the filthy rich, wet nurses to the soulless corporations."

"Yeah, right. Bunch of crap, but I see your point. Which is you can't do mental and physical harm to the innocent without paying the piper."

"Basis of the tort system."

"I'd say."

"Employers, corporations, builders, some politicians cry and moan about what they call huge settlements and are, in reality, chump change. People must be protected from abuse, accidental or otherwise. Many times there are no safeguards when they should be in place. If folks are not properly protected, well, lookee here, they must be compensated. Not all that complicated."

DeShales asked the waitress for coffee. Long past time to get back to work. Jensen, as always, awaited him. But the turn of the conversation fascinated him. He knew the odds were staggering against the coincidence theory; he was even convinced Zack knew it too. But friends, and the old admonition drilled into all lawyers – all people are entitled to legal representation, all are presumed innocent until – until what?

"This is so damn big, Zack. This is beyond big, it's a case for the law reviews."

"Easy, my friend."

"Anyway, I envy you, buddy. That's it, I offer both envy and congratulations, premature though they may be."

"I'm obliged."

"You must know, you got to know, this path is familiar, that I'm bursting with questions, about procedure, investigation, witnesses and, you know, other things."

"Sure, I know. Money. And we have walked this trail before."

"Can you blame me?" DeShales was practically pleading, curiosity a devouring factor.

"Hey, I've always leveled with you, just as you have with me. Always."

"Sure."

"Some of these matters, mostly the price tag, will be worked on in the next few days. Let's see, this is Tuesday. Let's meet here again on Friday. Like five P.M."

"Or four, if you can make it. I'm back in the saddle of being a whipped puppy. Home for dinner at six-thirty, part of the new deal. Armistice. Weapons stacked, ammo destroyed, know what I mean?"

"Four it is. And good luck on North by Northwest."

"At least it was a hell of a movie!"

Tom DeShales headed for the office, not with great anticipation. Here I am, lying to my best friend about my home situation. Like pearl divers, the kick to the surface for air was brief. Dinner at home, iceberg lettuce – what a farce.

There is definitely something wrong with me that I can't keep that filly in the barn. I remember I couldn't keep a honey very long in high school or college. Some guys have the touch of a safecracker, I've got the touch of a blacksmith. "Hang on, Tom baby, you're getting yourself down again. No way for a well known attorney to feel about himself." And so on, the rigors and uncertainties had undermined, through the years, his native resourcefulness. I'm lead, he though. Shirl is mercury. Am I finally getting through my thick skull that the two don't mix?

If I had my life to live over, I'd put my scope sight on a plain, loyal gal like Madge. My secretary would never do me like the present Mrs. And the BMW – I'm ashamed. No man should ever be reduced to bribing his own wife. Talk about unmanly, those expensive wheels represent a pitiful reaching out for something that has slipped away. I didn't have the ready cash on hand for the purchase. So, three years of big payments facing me on that sucker. What a bad joke I am.

He arrived at the office. Madge Johnson greeted him, as always, with a brilliant smile.

The Criminal Housewife

CHAPTER 13

"You got any idea what's up with Mom these days," asked Andy?

"Nothing's 'up' with her," said Meg. "I don't know what you're talking about."

"Come off it. You know damn well. I'm not as dumb as I look."

"Could've fooled me."

They sat together, brother and sister, best of pals, at McDonald's on an autumn afternoon. Andy, home for the weekend, Meg, with a rare Saturday off from the volunteer obsession. They wolfed the burgers, malts and fries and contemplated the changes in their lives.

"Aw, you're right, bro," said Meg. "Mom's changed and for the better. She seems, I don't know, more relaxed. She can be moody at times. Now, not a worry in the world."

"And with a busted wing, at that."

"She's on some kind of a shopping high. Spending dough like crazy."

"Well, the family, and the house, need stuff. Always have, come to think of it."

"We always been lower middle, manner of speaking. I never felt that way, but statistically."

"Where did you pick up that line of thinking?" Andy expressed amused shock.

"Helping build houses for folks poorer than we are. Or than we were. What are we now? I'm sure mixed up, but Dad still brings home some thin paper."

"Retail trade, the pits. But Dad likes it. Sell those nuts and bolts, cut those keys."

Meg suddenly became serious. She had invited her brother to go for food with her because she was worried about him, Andy, still rail thin.

"Mom gave you thirty thousand. Advanced you, loaned you - whatever. The idea was to get you off the chain gang and crack a book occasionally. Now you tell me it hasn't happened."

"Reality check, I guess."

"What the hell does that mean?"

"Watch your language, Kid."

"Shit. My language has got to be a lot better than those factory pals of yours."

"No doubt." But Andy was touched by his sister's genuine concern. They had always been close.

"I just don't know the score, Meg. Thirty thousand, like Captain Kidd's treasure. Maybe she borrowed it. Borrowed money has to be repaid. I bought a few things, mostly books, three month's rent, but I'm sitting on most of the dough for now. Look," he, too, was dead serious. "I'm going to cut back on outside work, that's a promise, but I'm worried about Mom and Dad."

"There's more."

"Yeah?"

"I'll be sixteen next summer. Driver's license time. Big wheels time. Race those rods up and down Main Street, you know how it goes."

"I never did much of that with the family car. But I sure as hell wanted to."

"Language, buddy." They laughed. Easy with each other, they treasured their time together.

"Anyway, I've hoped for years that, when the time came around, I could manage some kind of jalopy. Mom says 'no'."

"That's not all bad."

"You don't get it, bro. Now she's saying no load of scrap metal for her daughter. Nice wheels, not more than three years old and maybe, get this, brand new. Like a Mustang, something that neat."

"My God. If she said it she meant it. Mom doesn't lie."

"I know. Scary, huh?"

They finished their lunch, but tarried, the warm sunshine flowing through the windows of the Golden Arches, a gathering spot for the young in Crestburg.

"Let's recapitulate, as the profs say. This all started during the summer. First, out of a blue sky, Mom hit me with the big money transfer to my account."

"To get you off your tough work schedule."

"I know. I know."

"Then you get to thinking about it. You college guys think too much. Bad for the health."

"Tell me about it. I'm still bushed all the time like I've been the past year and more. But next semester, I'm making the break. Here's a handshake on that."

They clasped hands in the special way they had invented as children.

"It's downright noble of you, bro, to worry about the folks and the money. You're gone most of the time, I'm here and just as puzzled as you."

"I just about went out of my skull when I got the news of her injuries. Driving over to the hospital in Minneapolis, I wonder I didn't book a ticket." Andy shook his head. "I expected real devastation when we got in to see her. And there she was, sitting up in bed and watching T.V. Laughing and smiling like she didn't have a care in the world. She really put on a front for us, maybe not for the doctors or other people."

"Well, they had a lot of pain killer in her body at that time, I suppose."

"Still——"

"I know. That Mom of ours is tough. Tough as bone."

"Does her insurance cover everything?"

"Not a case of Mom's insurance, Kid. It's the airport's responsibility in their coverage. Mom won't have any medical out of her pocket or her insurance. I'm quite sure of that."

"Thanks, Mr. Attorney."

"Some day, Meg, I'll know a lot more about it. I'm aiming for business law, you know. Be available for small business, like Acme that I slave for. I don't think I'd be interested in working for huge corporations."

"My, aren't we exclusive. Maybe 3-M and places like that wouldn't be interested in you!"

Andy had a cocky grin. "Aw hell, they'll recruit me like I was Mr. America when the time comes! And what about you, less than two years of high school left? What then?"

"I'd been thinking the easy way out, Andy, because of finances. Take community college two years, then look around. That's what I was thinking up to this summer."

"Yeah. Now what?"

"Straight to the U, Engineering."

A wicked glint shone in Andy's eyes. "Women can't be engineers. Too tough." He yelped as a small fist drove into his biceps.

"I know you're kidding, Mr. Hotshot. I can show you dozens of structures within fifty miles of here. Housing projects, bridges, streetscapes, shopping malls, all engineered by the superior sex."

"I like your thinking, Squirt." He grinned. "When your jerry-built buildings fall down, I'll protect you in court."

"Thanks, loser. But back to Mom. She's either an unbelievable woman or the accident knocked something loose. She was so banged up around the face and neck. And that broken arm. She waves the cast around like it was a tennis racquet. Everybody signs it. And, I guess like you said, all paid for by big airport guys."

"It's the don't-give-a-damn attitude that has me puzzled. Yet, let's think of this: maybe it's not so strange. Is it possible that more money will be involved than paying the med bills?"

"What do you mean?"

"Damages. Comprehensive coverage, maybe litigation.

Payment for pain and suffering, mental stress, loss of income. That last one's a hoot!"

"Hey, are you just pre-law or into the real stuff already?"

Andy grinned, his smile a flash of white teeth in the booth. "If I'm going to be a lawyer, my mind has to start working that way."

Meg was pensive, glancing at her watch. Nearly time to leave.

"Your brain wave answers a lot of questions, bro. But, for us, we'll just yack about it. If we get too nosy, ask a lot of stuff, you know Mom. She'll have our hides."

"I've noticed. She sure guards her privacy."

"For sure. And her right to do so."

"Dad would know all this stuff. But we can't go behind Mom's back by grilling him."

"Gotta go, Andy. But first, for the most important thing, question of the day. When are you going to bring one of those coeds home for us to look over?"

"All in good time."

"It just may be that you're slower than molasses at the South Pole."

"Oh, I have my moments. Any special type you had in mind for me?" Andy grinned at her. "That is beyond living and breathing, like that?"

"That'd be a start. I'm not big on white, dark, background, ethnicity – "

"Ethnicity?" Andy howled. "Where the hell did you get that word?"

Meg smiled, a pure beam of sunshine in the nearly deserted McDonalds. "Social studies, I guess. We're big into that stuff now with all the Asians and Afros drifting into town. Wave of the future, my teacher days."

"Teacher knows best."

The Criminal Housewife

CHAPTER 14

"I feel like I'm watching a movie," said Tom DeShales, "a rented film that has to be returned tomorrow. And I can't get a grip on how the story ends. Help wanted."

"You're taking my latest case too seriously," offered Zack Taylor.

"I know I am. I'm hooked, like a teen age kid on sniffing glue. Have we known each other too long? Do I bleed when you get cut, all that sort of thing?"

"Possible. I know I sweat bullets when you tangle with guys like Jensen. I'm euphoric when you close a big deal. I feel like hell when you don't."

"Good thing we're not in the same partnership. My God, we'd spend all our time on emotional highs and lows."

"And that's not even counting our problems at home with our particular old ladies."

"Maybe we should swap."

Zack Taylor laughed. "We're a couple of smarmy old bastards, but wife swapping? I'm inclined to think that might be beyond even us."

"Guess so. You've got a peach of a wife, don't know what she sees in you."

"Of course you don't. No exhibitionist, me."

DeShales went on. "And Shirl's shaping up. She has become, matter of fact, quite a nice, compatible human being."

They drained their drinks, tap beer this time, and reordered, both giving a good natured hard time to the waitress.

"All this, leading up to the airport case. Anything new?" asked DeShales.

"The lady is recovering, slowly but steadily."

"At home?"

"Yeah, with daily treatments, physical therapy at the clinic. And some counseling."

"Wonderful."

"Cass will be O.K. physically. She's a tough gal, a real gamer. Still shook up, though. Twitchy, bad dreams, that sort of thing."

"Hell of an experience." DeShales grinned. "And blood brother, you know I'm out of my mind about the negotiations. The Boles deal was nothing compared to this. At least potential."

"We're talking ten mil."

"Nice talk."

"And we're girding our loins, if that isn't too biblical, to go to the wall on this." Zack was rueful. "I hate a trial, truth be known I'm not too sharp in the ring. When the bull charges, I'm not too slick with the cape."

"Know what you mean. I get a hollow feeling myself."

"That hollow feeling, like you're hung out to dry."

"Luck is involved, too," groaned DeShales. "Always seem to draw a sharp son of a bitch for an opponent. And judges, where do they get these guys? Cold eyed bastards, or bastardesses, as the case may be. Cut the heart right out of you."

"Well, as you know, I'm a coward who talks big. When I say we're willing to go to court, we're a hell of a lot better prepared to not go to court."

"Now you're talking sense, reality. Like cutting that ten mil in half?"

"Or more."

"How much more?"

Zack Taylor was bothered by a question he had asked himself a hundred times. How much, how little, the great battles of justice, wits and, mostly, nerve.

"In our minds, Mrs. Janes and I, we've pretty much decided on a Maginot Line."

"As I remember, the Maginot Line was breached. The wicked Fuhrer ran his tanks around the lines like scat backs."

"True. But follow through on that analogy."

"Say which?"

"The line was breached, true. But in the end, years later, the Nazis lost."

"See what you mean."

"We're not prepared, or in the mood, to drag this out for years. Even months. We've set our sights on the ultimate fallback, the no retreat, hold that line, absolute hardwood, laminated, carpeted floor. At three."

"I like your thinking. From the enemy's viewpoint, this should look like a sidewalk sale, compared to ten." Tom DeShales was into it now, enthused. "And, once again, the arithmetic is simple and beautiful. Could math ever become more elementary, two and one?"

"Thought you'd pick up on that."

"My lord, it's wonderful. And more important, I believe it's doable."

"Our feeling exactly." Zack drew a labored breath. "I'll admit to you, never to another soul, how goddamned scared I get, the insidious, creeping thought that we can't make the deal."

"You can do it, buddy. You and the blonde lady have so much going for you, all that trauma and injury."

"Yeah. And the injuries persist."

"Does that three include medical? The hypothetical three, that is."

"Hell, no, that's extra. All the medical, ambulance, Minneapolis Hospital and doctor costs and now the local costs, are being. picked up by the airport. The airport, which I might add, is making a great pitch on how concerned they are about all passengers, the warm-hearted bit. Big deal!"

"Big P.R. deal. But I'd do the same in their shoes."

"Naturally, so would I. But the whole medical, including physical and mental therapy, won't hit sixty thousand. So, no, doesn't affect the settlement." Zack sighed. "Ah, the settlement. I'll come out of this a depleted old wreck."

"But a pretty well-off wreck, I hope."

"I hope so, too." In the comfort of their favorite drinking spot, DeShales felt an overwhelming empathy for the brinksmanship of his friend. "You deserve it, Zack."

"I'm obliged."

"And there's that other thing. About lawyers and the general public. Fodder for the comedians. We take the gibes, the stale jokes, the general horseshit about rich attorneys. A guy has to take it with a smile but it makes me sick. Hell, I know a hundred lawyers, I mean really well, a couple hundred not so well."

"It's a tight circle."

DeShales went on. "And of all those, maybe half a dozen I'd call wealthy. A few more, what's the term, very affluent? Yeah. But most are struggling along like the butcher and the baker. High office expenses, tough collections at times."

"Tell me about it. A lawyer has to have a lawyer to collect the bills. Collect? At fifty cents on the dollar. Balls."

"And a lot of attorneys, the young ones, what a struggle. Wife working, or having kids, or both, the saints be praised. Paying off college loans. Fight, fight, A lot of them wish to hell they were back laying bricks or pounding nails."

"And young Mr. Janes wants to join the crowd. I wish him well."

They sipped their beers. Both were cutting down, Zack for weight, Tom for the truce with Shirl.

"Anyway," offered DeShales, "it's nice to see one of the good guys hit a real payday. Not wealth, don't want you spoiled, but sure as hell, at least lace curtain poverty."

"The Big P. Not poverty. Potential."

Another day, another autumn late afternoon in the warm confines of Michelle's bar and restaurant.

The lawyers were right about one thing. In the legal profession there were very few roads that led to wealth, Zack Taylor's activities, an exception. In Minnesota, doctors and developers and owners of large tracts of land were, as a rule, far more affluent. The loaded gentry, not from farming, all agriculture had been in the pits for years with corn and soybeans at prices at or below depression levels. But owning land near the burgeoning cities was better than a back yard oil well, without the uncertainty of the well going dry. The land owners could cherry pick, sell off twenty or forty acre parcels at a time and wait in noble leisure for the expanding market to come and meet them.

All this had been true for a decade in the metropolitan areas of Minneapolis/St. Paul where new malls and factories appeared, as if by magic, almost overnight. In Crestburg the same phenomena surfaced in a modified version. The same land that had lured the immigrant pioneers from Germany, Ireland and the Scandinavian nations to brave frontier harshness to stake out the quarter sections of the land grant era was now, field and woodland, sandy soil and loam, disappearing into the developer's earthmovers and pavers.

The beauty of the old countryside was gone in the rural areas lying in proximity to the city. Urban sprawl prevailed, although attempts to harness the sprawl were attempted. Crestburg, in another decade, would likely pass ninety thousand people, with no end in sight. For a minority of residents, this was big bucks country. For the clerks and teachers, the drivers and restaurant workers, steady jobs, but no bonanza.

But taking the good with the not so good, a wonderful place to live in, work and raise a family. Favorable aspects included great schools... public and otherwise... a moderately low crime rate, stable families, and cops and firemen that cared. The ragged uncertainty of the rust belt was not present here. There was a job for anyone who could drag the body out of bed to submit to the discipline of nine to five.

On the debit side of the ledger was, always, the climate. Winter brought cold, very cold, and frequent sub-zero temps that cracked radiators, froze water pipes and provided a decent living for those service folks who plowed snow and started cars immobilized into inert mounds of frozen metal and rubber. Spring could be sodden, summer hot and sultry, with squadrons of mosquitoes patrolling their sectors when the sun brushed the western horizon. Autumn, season of the angels, could be glorious in a palette of colors to rival, if not surpass, the leaf draped panoramas of Vermont and Maine. For the farmers, sunny harvesting or, conversely, dragging equipment through deluges of rain and sleet.

So, hardy people, in all walks of life, dealt with humor and good grace the vicissitudes and rewards of life in southern Minnesota. Most people loved the area and, still, in autumn, the autumn of their lives as well as the year, cheerfully said goodbye and joined the vast band of Midwesterners who became, some for months, many permanently, the snowbirds of Florida, Arizona and other sunbelt states.

And in those climes, they bragged incessantly on how things were done much better where they came from. "Ho boy, these slow moving natives," they would grumble. "Take all day to turn out work we'd have done by ten in the morning. And, by God, we'd do it right."

The Southern folks would yawn and smile and go on about their business, forgiving the boorishness of the paying invaders.

CHAPTER 15

Cassandra Janes lounged on the living room sofa. Her husband was comfortable in the recliner, reading the local daily paper. It might have been any evening of any day for the past decade. Homey, companionable. Cass felt a warm security, a sense of family. This adventure has not, as I feared might happen, torn us apart, she thought. I have never felt in my bones, including the one knitting in my forearm, more togetherness. Gale has been an angel in taking care of me. Of course, I can see that he's worried. He worries far too much. I've got to work on him about that.

She had been waiting for days for Gale to elaborate on his thoughts but he seemed in no particular hurry. Perhaps silence really is golden. Then she was surprised.

"What a handful you are, baby," he said laconically. "Here I send you off, not literally, to Chicago and with a few misgivings."

"You thought my old connections in Chi were a bit frayed, right?"

"Well, yes. But I worried, was concerned, I should say, about the wrong town. Hell, you never got out of the Minneapolis Airport. And how can anyone fly with a busted wing?"

"Skill and determination."

"What a crock. You never had the slightest intention of going to Chicago. Right?"

Cass considered, "Partially right, Mr. Holmes. I did all the prep activities. And, if things had gone wrong with my plan, if the timing was lousy, I'd still be in Chicago at this time."

"If things had gone wrong! Things did go wrong. You were injured, could have been killed."

"I know. And my life insurance is so pitiful," she chuckled. "You should provide more coverage for your klutzy wife. I tend to tip over, wearing anything but flats."

"Cass, don't give me that malarkey. It was all planned, wasn't it."

"The truth?"

"However much of the truth you can spare." Now Galen suddenly grinned. "You may not have a great deal of that commodity on hand."

"For you, hon, I have enough."

"My life's a wasteland of broken promises."

"Too bad for you. But, here goes. Of course it was all planned. And brilliantly, if I may be so modest. The cuts and bruises were factored in, not the fracture. That was a bit of overkill." She laughed freely, a refugee finally home. "What a deal. What went wrong made what went right even better."

"Better? Look at the cost."

"I had a broken leg once, when I was eleven years old. The doctor was amazed, said I knit like a garment factory. Well, old bones are not young bones, but the arm is doing great."

"And that's for me to know. Not the enemy."

"Gale, there is no enemy."

"Could have fooled me."

"I prefer a different term. Like adversary. Sounds nicer. Or merely the other party."

"Which possibly includes a cart driver who may lose his job. Or some clueless supervisor."

"I doubt that. Anyway, breaks of the game."

"I see." Galen shook his head in both disapproval and admiration. He could see that what he had predicted would be a disaster had not materialized. And his prediction had risen from a lack of knowledge on what form the scam would take. Who is this stranger that passes as my wife, and where did she acquire the traits and abilities, the iron nerve to handle such schemes? He had marveled at the nonchalant way Cass had pulled off the Boles department store operation. This was worlds beyond.

"Yeah, my arm feels better every day. As for the mental trauma, the hallucinations, the violent headaches, well, what do you think?"

"To be brutally frank, these matters are all negotiating ploys. A strange thing to say, hon. But, what the hell, you asked me."

"Of course I did. And of course you're exactly right. I must have inherited a tough constitution. I sleep like a baby. I haven't had head pains since the second day. But – my pride, my dignity, has been assaulted."

"I can see that. Ain't it awful?"

"The game didn't end when the cart rammed into me. That was only part one, actually the least important phase." The fire was back in her eyes, her color high in the lamplight of the modest living room. "Part two is ultimate reward time for Mr. and Mrs. Galen Janes."

"Not exactly, Cass. Leave me out of this."

"What do you mean?"

"What do you think I mean? Means I want no part of it, the settlement, whatever, if you ever actually get that far."

Cass exploded. Inwardly she had feared this – this holier than thou exclusion. She leaned toward her husband, her eyes hard slits.

"You son of a bitch. You sanctimonious bastard! This is a family, at least it has been until now. I put my body in great danger, my life on the line, if things had gone that far. For me, sure, we've been over that ground. But for Andy and Meg, too. And for you. You, my precious husband. Better or worse, sickness or health, all that bullshit." Her voice was higher now, bitter. "Now, you're out; well, if you're out of this, I'm out of your life. I won't stand for this treatment. I can hack a fractured arm, not a fractured family."

Galen, shaken, found his mouth dry, his emotions

stricken. Still, he managed a casual tone. "I see your point, Cass. This is all the family I ever want in this world. You know that."

"I thought I did."

"I've been tough on you because what you're into is tough business."

"What you are saying is, I'm a criminal. Sure I am, never claimed otherwise. I'm a greedy, self-centered, law-breaking scam artist. So what? I scam the public just like the big corporations and some of the politicians do. Those are my beliefs, always have been."

"I am well aware of your particular philosophy. I don't agree but there might be something in what you're saying." Galen paused, this was the crux of the matter. "It's just, how can I live the life of Riley, spend money all over the place, dough that I've never earned? I know that it's done all the time but it's a tough line for me to cross. I've given these things a lot of thought, ever since you launched this. Not all that simple, Cassandra."

She laughed, a derisive sound.

"Cassandra! What happened to Cass or are we getting a bit formal?"

From Galen, a quizzical grin. "Can we start over on this conversation?

"Of course. I blew my stack, hon. But I meant it, about the family bit. Richer or poorer, comes in the contract. We've been poor; we are going to be, trust me on this, rich. Together or separately. I'm in love with my husband so I prefer together. It just can't be both."

"Yah. I see."

"So far, just big words. Generalities. Let me put some meat on those bones. I'm talking a new life. Trips, big long trips to wonderful places I have never seen except on the travel channel or in National Geographic. A new house, new cars for both of us, new clothes. I helped out Andy with his finances. He'll need more, lots more, and so will Meg. But mostly you, Gale, you can't slave your life away at the same dead-end job. Nuts and bolts, locks and keys. You deserve better."

"You're getting to me, hon," he said. "I suppose if I had a sudden windfall, I'd want to share it with you, screw the origin. Can I be so stiff-necked to do otherwise, seeing as how I made no great effort to . . ."

"Stop me dead in my tracks."

"Yeah. And we're still talking about a hypothetical fortune. I can't imagine it'll be that easy."

"No, not easy. But you can bet every cow in the barn that it's a lock. Let's proceed from that point."

"Fair enough. I'm on board for everything you listed but one."

"Let me guess. The house."

"You got that right. I love this old shack. Needs work, I'll go along with that, like the roof. But this shady old street, wonderful old neighborhood, the trees, the garden. I could never trade this chunk of my life, our life, for one of those big, sterile boxes on a new yuppie street."

"We're yuppie generation ourselves."

"Age-wise, maybe." He ran his hand through thinning black hair, grey around the ears. "But the upwardly' mobile bit never got to me." He laughed, the storm was passing. "I have a few problems with your absolute trust in Zack Taylor, even though I like the guy."

"A few months back I threw in my lot with Mr. Taylor. Something like a marriage without the sexual perks."

"That's a mod viewpoint."

"I trust Zack because I have to trust him. I've watched him operate, worked right alongside. And so far, he's been great."

"He helps you pull off this deep dive, the man is another Clarence Darrow."

"Clarence who?"

"Forget it."

The Criminal Housewife

CHAPTER 16

"The holiday season can be brutal," sighed Tom DeShales. "Worst time of the year if you ask me."

"I wasn't about to," said Zack.

"Couple nights back, I'm trying to relax, watch the football game, and ghosts and goblins are banging on the door, shaking us down for candy. Little creeps, why the hell don't they stay home, do their homework? Skulk around the neighborhood, trick or treat. I'd like to give those little monsters a treat they'd remember!"

"And people think they've got it tough in Bolivia, Russia, places like that," said Zack. "They don't know what rugged is 'til they've endured Halloween in the U.S. of A. My heart bleeds for you, buddy. Those little kids have no business picking on you."

DeShales grinned sheepishly.

"Came on a little strong there, I guess."

"You got that right, Ebenezer."

"It's just, I'm a laid back guy. Not often laid but laid back."

"I understand the difference."

"And so I like the easy seasons, easy living. Summer, spring, early fall. Now after being whined and threatened out of coin and candy, Thanksgiving will be on us in a couple of weeks. More family turmoil and in-laws that should be in the funny papers."

"Now you're talking about my relatives."

"Then Christmas presents, what to buy the old lady so's to keep out of the doggie house."

"The eternal problem."

DeShales went on as though uninterrupted. "Then New Year's, where to go, what reservations to make. Raise hell, have fun, but don't get plastered. If the wife don't bust you, the cops will."

"That's what we pay them to do, citizen."

"I know, I know. But don't they ever let up?"

"This is the damnedest tale of unilateral hardship I've ever listened to." Zack grinned, he was enjoying every minute of his friend's discomfort. He had heard it all before in other years. "What can we do to ease the burden?"

"Order me another drink. Scotch and soda. I'm still safely within the Shirl limit."

"Done."

"And tell me the latest on your present field operation, the war between Cassandra and the airport moguls."

"Where did we leave off last time?"

"As I recall, at the round and shapely figure of ten. Ten to demand, three bottom dollar. Or do I disremember? Monetary sums that stratospheric give me a nosebleed, air is thin, I gasp for oxygen."

"Get off," said Zack. "You dicker in real estate developments that run into forty, fifty million. You know more about strings of zeros than I ever will. I'm just a mouthpiece."

"Not so." DeShales was grumpy. "That forty, fifty stuff is for the developer. I just try to finagle the deal with the bankers, for a pittance. You know bankers, don't you? Six hundred dollar suits and rusty carburetors in the chest cavity where some of us have hearts."

"I have met a few. And I've listened to the same sad refrain. 'We'd like to help you, Mr. Taylor, really we would, but we are, after all, responsible to our shareholders.' Like that. Like they don't own most of the stock themselves."

"Can we get back to the lady, the blonde with the shattered arm and spirits?"

"I'm in that no man's land of squalls ahead."

"Meaning?"

"It looks like my worst fears are going to be realized after all. The hopeful out of Court."

"So, District Court, Minneapolis?"

"The date has been set, mid-December."

DeShales whistled, "that soon?" He was shocked at the swift movement of justice, something he was unaccustomed to in year-long housing deals.

"None too soon for me."

"Got the jitters?"

"Truth be known, yes. But you know the drill from school days. Make up for it with thorough preparation and a solid courtroom plan. Might have to go for consultant help on this. Not you, buddy, much as I'd like that."

"Thanks. But you're right. If you take on associate help it has to be a heavy hitter in that line of work. I'm real estate, be useless as a fly rod in Death Valley."

"Jelly legs or not, I'll kill those Ivy Leaguers in Court. I'll bury them."

"That's the spirit. And you've got the solid case. They've got bullshit. The woman should have been, more careful, worn sensible shoes, all that crap."

"I'll moider the bums."

Tom DeShales grinned. "Way to go buddy. In the meantime let's have another drink. I'm approaching the Shirl line of demarcation. But I'm not there yet."

"When you cross that line, I'll be there."

"Thanks, buddy. Will you come to the funeral?"

"Possibly. Depends what I'm doing that day. Winter time is slow. That's my best schedule. Summer time, I don't know. If it interferes with golf or fishing, forget it. I will send a card though."

"Hallmark?"

"You got it. Nothing less." Zack was serious. "But you worry me, Tom. You can't die or get done in by Shirl. It can't work."

"How's that?"

"The funeral. You haven't got six friends!"

Zack Taylor drove home. Tom DeShales' good natured grumbling about the coming holiday season had stirred emotions within the hard-boiled attorney that were always banked, always ready to spring into flames of dark despair. The holidays, when families gather together in a closeness that crowned the diversities of the year, weighed upon him. The family, himself and Jan and the one child who had, after many years, blessed their home eight years before.

So each year, around this time, the dull ache moved in, sometimes stilling his breath. He knew that at Christmas time, in spite of elaborate presents, it would be even worse. The joy and anticipation on children's faces, so familiar to him with his nieces and nephews, was a thrust to the heart. Billy was as quiet and impassive about gifts and special visits as he was about everything. Life, precious and often exciting to Zack and Jan, was to this child a dull, flat, colorless plain. The local clinic, renowned though it was, had shadowed the case for years, since that terrible period in the toddler stage when the symptoms, finally, became too acute to ignore.

Zack shook off the dark vapors as he entered the house. Years of discipline had honed his ability to be what he must for Jan and Billy.

"Hi ya, baby," he boomed to his wife. Zack grabbed a quick kiss and lifted the solemn Billy in his arms, ruffled his tawny hair and hugged him. The boy stared at him with solemn, unblinking eyes.

"Tough day, honey?" she asked. Jan was busy with slow baked chops, his favorite.

"Oh, sure, they're all tough. But you know me, I like 'em that way."

"Because, linebacker, you're even tougher. I know the routine."

"Well, I've been telling myself that for a long time,

darling. But this time of year, you know how I get."

"You look normal to me. Normal for a grizzly."

They sat down to dinner, Billy between them, silent, detached, very polite. "What does he think?," wondered Zack. Perhaps more than we can even imagine, we haven't been there. Billy's appetite was healthy. Home schooling, such as was possible, and home cooking helped. But, thought Zack, there will be bridges to cross, so many difficult decisions to be made in the future, barring a miracle breakthrough from the labs.

"Any new cases?" asked Jan. "Or still wrapped up exclusively in the big one?"

"Pretty much. Had a fender bender in the downtown area might develop into something. Clear violation on the other guy's part, maybe a whiplash on my guy. We'll see." He relished his food. "Man, some chops, Best ever."

"Thank you, dear. When you wolf your food, I know I did something right."

"I don't wolf my chops. I'm an athlete. I eat slowly and sensibly."

"Another Jim Thorpe, without the medals." Jan touched her son's shoulder softly. "Try to sit up straight, Billy. You are so much handsomer when you're not slouching." The boy's eyes remained vacant, but there was a discernible shift in his position.

How does she do it, Zack wondered. Not much contact, but some, and I can never break through.

"The big one, as you call it," he murmured, "is big for my client, huge for us. For myself, not all that important." He stopped, disliking insincerity. "Check that statement, it's a bald-faced lie."

"But for you and Billy – everything." Zack did his best to show a cheerful smile. "We'll get through this holiday season OK, hon. And, if the money rolls in, who knows what the New Year will bring? We may have the moola to pursue this thing all the way. There are other medical institutions, other researchers, other – who knows?"

"Billy's future, it seems, may be in the hands of

Cassandra Janes. And, of course, her brilliant attorney."

"Now you sound like DeShales."

"Is that bad?"

"What do you think? The man is one hundred percent B.S."

Jan laughed. "You guys, what a pair. If you're not insulting each other directly, you're doing it third person. I'm not certain you could exist without Tom as a sounding board."

"It'd be tough."

The Taylor family finished the meal. Zack took a casual look at the local paper. Then the national savior of troubled households, the black box, took over. As the manic banter of 'Friends' rolled off the screen, Zack monitored Billy closely. He could see, as always, no change, had no idea if the vacant eyes followed the action on the small screen.

At bed time, Zack carried the eight year old upstairs. Not a good idea, he knew. They had been given all the current counseling on not treating the boy like a helpless baby. But the holiday melancholy engulfed him and he felt compelled. He tucked the boy in, kissed him and went back to his wife, his mind, as so often, a strange mixture of hope and quiet desperation.

This is your life, Zack Taylor. A good enough life, with a strange twist of fate, he thought. But I'm a tiger, as DeShales says, and with financial success in the possible future, I'll make this life all it can be. Who knows, Billy may yet discover and experience the beauty and wonder of the world.

I was not kidding when I told Jan that the present case with Mrs. Janes holds our future in its legalistic hands as well as the future for Cass and her family. Those kids, Andy and Meg, are the best. Can they remain untarnished by the operations of their Mom? I hope so, although there isn't much the wily lawyer can do about that.

The price of friendship took over his thoughts. Why

am I so blessed and Tom DeShales so torn up and disjointed? The man is about as removed from the ordered ranks of angels as anyone I know. He is a slob, often inefficient in his legal research, or so I have been told by others, thin skinned with a streak of paranoia a yard wide. The man has never revealed to me his feelings, that as a cuckold he is somehow unworthy, but the feeling is in my bones that he is truly a cuckold or, just as destructive, imagines he is.

I've heard from others that he has actually become, not an actual stalker, but a skulker, shadowing Shirl's comings and goings, constantly searching for clues that will prove her errant behavior. How can a guy, a terrific person like Tom, sink to that level?

Without being educated in the science of human behaviorism, I believe I know the answer and it is gradualism. A good marriage doesn't turn sour overnight or in a month or year. It just creeps along the slow and tortuous path toward dissolution. Fatigue is as common in unions as bickering, far more familiar to the courts and counselors than violence.

That's how I see my buddy's predicament at this dangerous stage of life. It is as common as a head cold and aspirin won't help either one. Shirl, bored and discontent leaves, comes back, leaves again, perhaps not physically, but her heart and passion dwell in other places than the big house on Summit Hill. She has the urge and the cruelty to cast a wider net. If Tom's time of life is a tortured stage of uncertainty, certainly so is hers. Some women feel that fate gave them a backhand slap; they missed the big pleasure cruise and are determined to catch a later ship. It is a tough situation. I'm lucky and blessed with Jan but, if the situation were reversed, I'd be strung out too. For a while. Then my hot temper would explode and who knows what might happen.

Hang in there, Tom DeShales, old friend. Things may get worse before they get better, but eventually you'll find a better deal. Maybe with that secretary of yours. Unmarried, with a clean slate? She's really a honey and strikes me as a gal that's as true blue as a summer sky.

The Criminal Housewife

CHAPTER 17

The days of autumn that dragged on for the attorney were just as slow for the residents of 407 Cravath Lane. The downspouts and gutters had been cleared of a summer's debris, the leaves raked and raked again as the hardwood and softwood of their own and neighbors trees followed their own particular rhythms of the seasons. Squirrels chattered about the lawns and stored nuts and acorns in mysterious caches. A few strips of new caulking had been applied to old fissures around doors and window frames. Storm windows had been washed and hung.

Galen Janes went about these homeowner tasks with his usual efficiency. His mind was aflame with possibilities, with the unknown future his talks with Cassandra had unfolded. The house had been, in the end, the only real contentious issue and he felt he was prevailing in that matter. The financial figures, unknown and as yet uncounted, he had attempted to dismiss as fantasy. He knew the fresh windfall was a bare possibility but Galen could not force himself to an acceptance. And so he busied himself, as he did every November, to keep a respectable appearance on the old house exterior and warmth and comfort inside.

I have to keep a cool head on all this disturbance, my wife's unbelievable move to stratagems beyond my reckoning, he thought. This mad adventure, balanced on a razor edge between prosecution and fulfillment has certainly, if nothing else, brought my life a new excitement. Perhaps I should be grateful for that. Dullness, I know, has increasingly engulfed me.

He removed old worn and cracked squares of tile for a

patio enlargement project. Cass, in jeans and red sweater, joined him as he bent to his work.

"You've been quiet lately, Gale." Just conversation, the woman was relaxed as always. "Can you use a cuppa, you've been going pretty steady?"

"I'm a beaver. Got to repair the dam."

"Damn right. And fill the root cellar, mend the sod walls. Giant in the earth, baby."

"You ain't a lot of help."

"I am, as you well know, incapacitated by severe and life threatening injuries."

"Looking at you, I keep forgetting. Pro fighters should be in as good shape."

"Looks will fool you. I play with pain."

Galen burst out laughing. What do you do with a person like that? Fat and sassy and poised on a stick of dynamite. A marvel.

Cass pulled up a chair, then another. She went back to the kitchen for two coffees.

"Tinge in the air, Gale. Lemonade season is over 'til April."

Galen took the steaming cup, with a nod. She studied him, her plain and perfect mate.

"You haven't asked me a thing lately. In fact, not for weeks."

"I know. Somehow I figured, what the hell, your deal. I should butt out, not screw things up."

Cassandra spoke fondly. "Aw, you wouldn't screw up, hon, you might even help. You're really a lot smarter than I am. In every way."

"I flunked out of scam school."

She laughed. "Well I passed, with top grades. At least up to this point."

"Are you in that no-man's land of waiting, hoping?"

"I guess. But I had no great expectations for a real swifty. Hell, I don't know what I expected... it's all new ground, virgin soil, if the expression fits." Cassandra lighted two Marlboros and passed one on. "Naturally, I'd have loved a quick resolution. Now, the tough get tougher, know what I mean?"

"Sure. And Zack?"

"Don't worry about Mr. Taylor. He's everything you said. A tiger."

"An endangered species." He laughed, remembering tough racquet ball encounters. "But he'll battle all the way for you. That's one good thing."

"Gale, we got a lot of good things already. Andy is set for the rest of college. Meg has new clothes and her own TV at last. Next year she'll get her driver's license so I'll be getting her a good used car. I'm happy. And I sure hope you are."

"I'm trying to hang on, Cass. I go to work, I come home, all the regular stuff. But the deck is shifting under my feet."

"Aw, what the hell. Trying times for now and you, the innocent guy, caught in the middle."

"I could've abandoned ship when all this started. When Boles got careless with their merchandise."

"But you didn't, hon. You stuck by me when you thought I might get nailed. I didn't and I won't."

"You're beyond belief."

"Next spring, when we slip onto that plane for England, Italy and points east and west, we'll start a new life. I'll prove to you, something I've wanted to prove for years."

"Such as?"

"That I'm not a witless, uneducated blonde, but a serious citizen of the world."

"All that sounds great. Take that plane east, the opposite direction from the one to Nam twenty odd years ago. Back when you were attempting to be the new Gloria S."

"I couldn't shine her shoes then, I was all talk. I've changed, not all my beliefs on how this country is manipulated, I'm about the same on that. But now I'm all action."

"More action than I can handle."

"Talk is cheap, unless you're a lawyer, like the brilliant Zack Taylor."

"Zack has his problems. And tremendous expenses with that poor kid."

"What are you talking about, what kid?"

"I can't believe he hasn't leveled with you about his 'special' child."

"Mr. Taylor has been all business. I don't know a thing about his personal life. Except he wins at poker and slams you in racquetball."

"He lies like a rug, at least on one of those counts, likely both. If a man will lie about sports, he'll lie about gambling."

"It's not lying. It's macho. All you guys are infected with the same virus, no antidote in sight." But Cassandra was concerned. "What about the kid? I swear it's news to me."

"His boy, around eight, is autistic."

The news shook Cass. She had not known, even guessed, about such a possibility.

"So," said Galen, "while I might or might not enjoy some side benefits from your egalitarian hobby, I hope like hell there's something in it for Zack. The burden has been heavy financially. And emotionally, beyond comprehension."

"I'd think so."

"From what I know, which isn't a lot, the Taylor's handle it well. And it speaks to his bulldog determination."

Now Cassandra was dead serious, her jaw set. "This makes me all the more determined that a decent payday is ahead for Mr. and Mrs. Zack Taylor."

"That's a nice thing to say. Just when I have you pegged as the woman with a heart of flintstone, you show a caring side."

"I'm still tough, baby, you'd have to turn me on a spit for twelve hours before you could get a fork in me."

Cassandra was defensive now. "But you know how I am about kids. That's a different story."

"Could've happened to us, to anyone. We've been lucky in that aspect of life."

"We've been lucky in a lot of ways, hon. Now get back to work, you slacker!"

She kissed him, one good arm around his neck, the damaged arm in a sling close to her side. The deep kiss held promise that her golden injuries would never prevent later fulfilling.

Galen studied the patio project. The discarded squares were of a dull blue-grey. A new day dawning, new colors, he thought. I'll get down to Home Depot and pick up some tile of brick red or even yellow. Flaunting colors for a strange family that flaunts the rules.

The money, Christ, the money. We've already hit on the Boles surrender, at least for the kids. If this new dream of Cass' becomes reality, this weak-kneed hypocrite will be faced with decisions almost as tough as what grunts to send out on patrol.

Thoughts of Nam and his buddies, Nick and Larry, clouded his mind, as usually happened in his times of stress. Larry had surrendered his life, his body blown apart by a land mine, and had died instantly, a poet's voice stilled forever. Nick Evans, bluff, tough and unbeatable, had survived and retreated after discharge to his mountain retreat in Tennessee, taking up his natural trade of running moonshine to what he called, "the trade."

Galen made the pilgrimage to the mountains a few years before to enlist Nick's help and his knowledge of explosives in a jewelry heist. The operation, thanks to the mountain man's help, had been successful, the money freeing Andy, finally, from indebtedness. Galen had fallen in love with the Tennessee mountains and come very near to falling in love with Nick's sister, Samantha. The twice divorced woman, mother of two terrific boys, had been smitten, partly by Galen's charm, partly, he suspected from pure loneliness. Only his enduring, lifelong adoration of his wife had pulled Galen back from the brink of a doomed affair.

Why am I haunted by these memories, he wondered? Are the latest turmoils of my life the force that propels me to wish that Nick was here? The ex-sergeant's counsel had helped him survive Vietnam, had aided him in his own particular lawlessness. Could that burly figure help him now? Should I venture again to that faraway spot, a world removed from this bustling Midwest area, his home now and for the remainder of his time on earth.

Galen thought deeply about the possibility, then put the notion aside. I'll work this problem out alone. Nick Evans has as much larceny in his soul as my devoted wife. Do you enlist an arsonist to help put out the fire?

I'm paying the price of being such a loner all my life. Know a lot of guys but close friendship in this town has never been easy for me. Guys at work, they're OK but I never have them over to the house for a beer. Cass and I have never double dated since some unfortunate attempts years ago.

I go to work at the store, I do my bit of farming in the garden, tinker with the house and my shop in the basement. Hunt and fish, usually alone, unless I can talk Andy into it when he's around.

Somehow that war in Nam cut me off from the warmth of the human race. I can't seem to find my way back, my fault, because truth be known, I haven't really tried. No wonder I'm so dependent on Cass and, being dependent, have always overlooked her faults. She has them, but they're as precious to me as her virtues.

CHAPTER 18

Dreams. There are the impossible ones, lottery winnings, cruises to the Caribbean and Greece, a plush job at seventy grand per annum. Foolish meandering dreams that are only a waste of time, a perversion of one-upmanship. And then there are the practical dreams. A decent job, a loving family, a roof over your head and groceries in the fridge and pantry. These are the dreams I hope to help with, the down to earth yearnings of people down on their luck.

So went the thoughts of Meg Janes as she pulled two by fours from the lumber truck and piled them neatly in rows alongside the completed block basement. She worked with the framing lumber and sacks of nails and other construction hardware. The four by eight plywood sheets were too heavy and difficult to handle for her. That unloading would wait until one of the carpenters had time to help.

It was past four in the P.M., her last class had finished at two. Meg was healthy, happy, windburned and dog tired. She knew she could be logging hours at the drive-in; she had worked to ten the night before and could use the money. But Habitat for Humanity called for sacrifice, a combination of tradesmen, week enders, old folks and the occasional kid – the gofer, the helper of last resort.

"How did I ever luck into a gig like this?" She talked to herself as she busied herself with the tasks at hand. No one to hear, she worked unsupervised at the moment. This often happened. In an enterprise dependent on volunteers, the people who worked on the projects came and went as their schedules and other commitments allowed. Do I have some kind of calling, she wondered, like the guys and gals who go into the religious life?

Haven't felt that touch on my shoulder. I only know that this work suits me and the feeling constantly takes away my breath. There is no sacrifice.

She glanced at her watch, time to get moving. Lately, Meg had been helping more at home. And the conversation with Andy still bothered her. A talk with Dad is in order, she. thought. She jumped on her bike and pedaled toward home, two miles across town from the building site. Meg had assumed more of the household chores and the cooking since her mother's accident in the airport.

The December air was raw even though the sun still streaked through a low sky in the Southwest. But Habitat for Humanity plugged along in all seasons, the supply never catching up with the need.

"Dad," said Meg. "Did you ever break a confidence, a promise?"

Galen gave Meg a skeptical look. "Hey, true confessions time, hon?"

"Sort of."

"So, why do you ask?"

They sat together in the kitchen nook at home. Midweek, Andy back at the U, Cassandra shopping, still with the left arm in a sling, the cast removed.

"I had kind of an agreement with Andy," said Meg. "Now I feel like breaking it."

"I see."

"We've been worried about Mom."

"She's doing fine. Not to worry."

Meg was not to be put off. "I know, the arm. And her face looks perfect again. I don't mean that."

Galen felt the sudden weight of a loving family member closing in. He had worried about this, now he wondered, can I handle this?

"Andy and I, well it's just between us. Thirty thousand to Andy, which he sure needed even though he hasn't followed through yet."

"You mean on the work load?"

140

"Yeah, he's kind of afraid. Scared that this is all coming down."

"He shouldn't worry, honey. Neither should you, the money is there."

"I'm sure it is. I don't know why I'm sure, but Mom wouldn't hang us out to dry."

Galen nodded. He walked to the fridge for cokes for both of them. A stall. He didn't care for soft drinks.

"Where does the broken confidence come in?"

"Well, with you. Mom made it plain the money was none of our biz. Then we agreed it wouldn't be fair to bug you. Yeah, we agreed. But I changed my mind, which is wrong."

"That's not so bad, honey. People do change their minds. All the time." He snapped the tabs and poured the cokes into water glasses. "Drink up."

"You don't even like coke, you old faker."

Galen laughed in relief. His irreverent, tough as nails daughter was in form. "Well, this is turning into a special occasion. They'll be thanking us in Atlanta." He feigned appreciation. "So, if you are so inclined, break the confidence. What can I do for you?"

"I don't know, Dad. Tell me what's going on, I guess. This is family, after all."

Galen stroked his chin while silently agreeing. He reflected the parameters of his word, his duty to his wife, his obligation to his kids.

"I'm sure you are familiar with the word 'dilemma.'"

"Well, duh!"

"You had a confidence with your brother. And you know how I love the fact you two are close."

"Pretty much. But he can be a dink."

"He's a college boy, goes with the territory."

"I suppose."

Galen eyed his daughter and wondered again. How had he helped produce such a gem?

"Your Mom, I assume, told you she ripped off a jewelry store, made a killing on Wall Street, some such

B.S.?"

"In a kidding way. But when she said butt out, she was dead serious."

"I imagine. Back to the struggle, the dilemma. I do know, partly, what is going on. Some local outfit, I can't tell you which one, made a false charge against your mother. Then they recanted, with a certain amount of – gratuity. For her cooperation."

"They strong arm her, give her the busted arm? No, wait, that happened out of town, in Minneapolis. What's the connection?"

"None, that I know of. No, the arm, the other injuries, pure accident. Could happen to anyone."

"Are we getting anywhere here, Dad?"

"Hang on, kid. I'm doing my best. You see, I'm locked in on the confidentiality bit too with your Mom. But it's not so stringent as you might think."

"As I might think?" Meg was getting restless. "How the hell – excuse me Dad, how do I know what to think right now?"

Galen was unperturbed. "It's not a water-tight agreement I have with your Mom. Because she deliberately, and I might say, thankfully, left me out of the picture. She knew I really preferred to be left out because I hate to get involved in legal entanglements, and legalities seemed possible. She knows that's a kind of hang-up I have."

Meg thought about this information, sipping her coke, holding the glass with a hand that displayed fingernails ungroomed, visible evidence of hard, gritty work on the housing projects.

"I guess I'm really glad you're not in a position to tell me more." She grinned. "Makes me feel better."

"Fine. I guess."

"Because, well, if it's not too disrespectful – "

"Perish the thought."

"If it's not too disrespectful," Meg went on, "it kind of is a bond. Between us. I don't really know what's coming down, neither do you."

"Fellow dummies."

Meg hugged her father and rumpled his thinning hair, the gray sprinkled about the ears.

"I love you, Dad. And I sure love Mom just as much. I just worry about a family that keeps things from each other."

"That's a wonderful attitude, baby. You were always bright, right from day one. You brother had just turned five when you showed up. We had about given up, we both wanted a little girl so bad. About ready to hit the adoption route. You must have known that, just got in under the wire. Now you worry about the poor and destitute." Galen chuckled. "Andy caused us a lot of worry in his high school days, doing drugs, selling 'em. You never gave us a sleepless night."

"Oh, I've done a lot of stuff you and Mom don't even know about."

"Such as?"

"Hey, I can have my secrets, too, you know."

"Fair enough. Build those houses. Just don't get involved with some low life skinhead with a dozen tattoos and a ring in his nose. Your Mom and I have tried to steer you right. Hope we've succeeded."

"Oh, I know where it's at, Dad. You needn't worry. Anyway, I like 'em with long hair and plastered to an electric guitar." Meg giggled, a trace of the little girl returning. "And they better know how to pound a nail straight. I don't go for spoiled mama's boys."

"Somehow, don't know just why, I find that a bit encouraging."

"Heck, I'm just a kid, Dad. Worry about Andy. He works too hard, the guy's neglecting the ladies."

"I'll speak to him."

"Hey, do that." Meg left the kitchen nook and proceeded to start preparations for dinner knowing her mother would likely be late.

Later, Galen resumed the inner struggles that had for

months haunted him. He had used the word "dilemma" with his daughter, but that word now seemed inadequate to the problems of his life. Forces of good and evil bedeviled him. He would not lie to his children – he could not tell them the truth. His pledge to Cassandra rested on a foundation of sand, they had not factored into their agreement the natural curiosity of intelligent children.

Galen felt he had not handled the dialogue with Meg in a competent manner. Andy, with his pre-law foundation, would pose an even greater challenge unless he decided to let sleeping dogs lie.

Irony had always helped in traumas of the past. And so, Galen thought, I screwed this up royally. If money is the root of all evil, I've got a blooming root cellar going here. There must be a graceful way out, but I'm not a very graceful man. I blunder, I stall and I didn't really answer, truthfully, Meg's questions. I think that kid saw through me like an X-ray.

I am grateful that, for now, she didn't bring up the matter of Zack Taylor and how come this man is suddenly in our lives. Andy and Meg, near as I know, have no inkling of the subtle, behind the scenes, legalities that attended the Boles matter and what part Zack played. Thank God for small blessings, he thought. His natural wryness returning, he considered, is one hundred and forty grand a small blessing or a large one? Cassandra, I know, considers it just an appetizer, the main dish still to come. I'm fearful, but powerless. What is to happen will happen.

And I've been increasingly thinking again of Nick Evans, but I'm afraid it's bad thinking, trying to patch up the present with the past. The mountain man was of tremendous help to me years back. Now I fight alone and that is the way it has to be. If I can't handle my own conflicts, I'm not sure I deserve a family – two great kids and a wild wife.

The Criminal Housewife

CHAPTER 19

They hauled the heavy metal auger across the ice
together. Zack Taylor, plowing ahead without a thought,
Tom DeShales walking on eggshells, constantly testing
the ice of Lake Pepin for strength.

"I know we had a couple zero nights," said DeShales.
"But lake ice is tricky. I'm having second thoughts."

"Aw hell, thinking isn't your long suit. Let's get the
damn hole bored."

DeShales grumbled but went along. "Remember," he
said, "last spring one time, same beautiful lake, we
wondered about guys going through this ice in their
snow machine toys. Remember?"

"How can I remember that? You gab so much I'd need
a tape recorder to file it all."

"Well, we did. Now, here we are, doing the same fool
thing. Are we nuts?"

"Half of us are. I'm fine."

They found what seemed, based on past years'
experience, a decent spot. The auger started with the
first pull and chewed its way through the ice. Tom
DeShales was relieved to see a full five inches deep in
the bore hole. They put down a second hole and baited
the hooks with minnows.

"See," said Zack. "More than enough. Plenty ample ice
for two skinny guys like us."

"Maybe."

"You see, lard, you got us mixed up with
snowmobiles, pickup trucks, stuff like that. It's not just

the weight but the forward action of a vehicle that makes it dangerous on ice."

Zack dropped his line in one hole, DeShales followed suit in the second.

"Aw, hell, Tom, I don't want you to worry. Four inches can hold us, you've just forgotten. This looks like at least five or six. Been a bitch of a cold spell this early."

"You're right, Zack. What a frigid mother. I'm surprised you could get away with all that's on your plate these days."

Zack hunkered on his haunches, his down lined coveralls warming him; he was content. Eight degrees, the mentality of the ice fisherman is a wondrous thing. The winter air was calm.

"I'm here, Tom, for two reasons. First, buddy, because you were good enough to come along although this isn't exactly your dish. But you're a trooper and I appreciate it."

"This isn't summer fishing for damn sure. But it's fishing. We go with what the calendar gives us."

"Second reason," said Zack. "I'm here because I should be in Minneapolis. They set up another meeting. I said, can't make it, previous engagement that I had somehow overlooked."

"Strategy move, huh?"

"Naturally. I'm toughing it out. I have to restrain myself, the old backbone bit. I feel things are going well, but I can't be certain. And I sure as hell can't appear eager. Too much at stake. I may be way off base, my thinking. But I sure need the therapy of the outdoors, this clean cold air and the peaceful feeling of fishing. Man – just crouching here, dropping a line. Brings perspective. Know what I mean?"

"Rough game you're in, Zack. You've got to go with your gut feeling."

"Yeah." They fished in silence for a quarter hour and were rewarded with a couple of keepers.

"I'm up against some big time pros in this damage

matter, Tom. And stiffing them on a meeting date won't fool them, that I know. But it might keep them unsettled, get them to quarreling among themselves. Dissension – man, how I long for dissension in that smarmy group of superior honchos."

"Might work, can't hurt. Sounds like you're keeping your cool in the negotiations."

"Cool as this frozen pike, Senator. And this beauty is a good sixteen inches."

The rotund DeShales, also insulated in a goosedown suit, was getting into the mood. Not a natural for this type of activity, he was happy to be along, knowing that Zack Taylor's need to brush off the legal cobwebs with the purification of cold air was real.

"How long till your Court date?"

"Five days. Next Tuesday."

"Will your star witness be called?"

Zack pondered this. "Not sure but we're set if she is." A sardonic grin, "Boy, are we ready! I've rehearsed her like a Broadway star. Hour after hour. I've been merciless."

"She can cut the mustard?"

"Never saw anything like it. I've praised her, insulted her, humiliated her, savaged her. I've used every trick I possess to break her. The woman is amazing. I can't get to her. I'm damn sure the opposition can't crack her, either."

"Yeah? Sounds good. But office pretend interrogation and on the stand, two different animals."

"I know, I know. But this lady is in complete control. The right dignity, the proper controlled anger at what has been done to her. And, the envelope please, a kind of poignancy you have to witness to appreciate. Not too heavy, not too contrived."

"You could sell tickets."

Zack laughed. He was discovering the freedom from tension he needed.

"Cassandra Janes is primed and ready for a

performance that I pray she'll never have to give. It's all preparation, of course, all contingencies anticipated. Just in case."

"Execute the drill, sure."

"The doctors' testimony and the visual marks, still slightly visible on Cassandra's face without makeup, plus carefully favoring the left arm as she moves about, should be more than sufficient."

"Witnesses available?"

"And eager to testify. Two of them, especially an older gentleman and his wife. They just can't get over the spectacle of that shoe stuck in the carpet."

"Talk about the proverbial ace in the hole. That hole card is tremendous."

The fishing was good. The cold carcasses laid out on the ice were adding up to a decent haul. Tom brought up an old sore point. "Exactly when are we going to give in to the thrust of modernism and get us a shack? They're not all that darn expensive."

"Exactly never, far as I'm concerned, although I am regionally celebrated as a compromiser."

"Celebrated? Not by me."

"We've been over this before, my upholstered friend. Ice fishing, in the open, is for men. Real men. Shack fishing is for the effete."

"Color me effete."

"Aw, you're tough, Kid. But it's the time factor more than anything else. Fighting the clock, you know. We're out here a couple hours and we're ready to head for town and surround a couple drinks. In a shack, you're much too comfortable. No wind, maybe a kerosene heater, six pack or two, sandwiches and so on. When would you get your lawyering done? Who'd ever want to leave to get back home?"

DeShales was morose. "Who indeed?"

"Another thing about the damn shacks. They don't just magically appear and disappear. Haul them up from town on a trailer. Haul them out on the ice. Haul them off in late winter when the word comes down from the bureaucrats. And maybe your shack gets vandalized when you aren't around."

"How the hell do you vandalize a shack? Most squatters might improve the ones I've seen."

"Possibly. But to get back to the time factor. We ain't kids, Tom, but we sure as hell are not like some of those creaking antiques we see out here. Old guys, got nothing to do but fish. Fish and then lie about it."

"I'm not above lying myself."

"Tell me about it. Those old guys sit in those shacks, some shacks handmade, some factory jobs, all the comforts of home and none of the static. Just sit and fish and eat and drink beer and break wind, go outside to take a leak, some don't even do that, I've been told. Sanitation suffers in ice shacks."

"Get off. These are solid, respected senior citizens, backbone of the nation. Some of 'em war heroes. And Zack Taylor slanders them. Just to get me to agree not to go halves on a decent shack, get us out of the cold."

Zack grinned, satanically. "You're onto me. Might have known couldn't fool a sharpie like you." His laugh rang out in the frigid air.

"I'm happy you're amused. But we still need a shack. If not this season, next season for sure. My knees are giving up the fight. Help wanted."

"You could be right. I promise I'll think about it. For now, we're out of here."

Zack Taylor felt the serenity he had sought. The specter of negotiations, arguments, fine points of law and looming court battles vanished. This has been perfect, he thought, a cleansing of the body, a healing of the soul in the bosom of nature, a defying of what the elements could muster.

To an extent the wind, dormant earlier, was freshening. Windburn, as much a hazard in winter months as sunburn in hot weather, was to be avoided. The two lawyers packed the catch into a knapsack which

DeShales carried. Zack Taylor shouldered the auger and the two stalwarts headed for the shore, their car and the forty mile drive, through the beauty of a winter day, back to Crestburg.

CHAPTER 20

One week before Christmas the two attorneys sought relief from swirling snow and zero temperatures to warm their spirits in the friendly confines of Michelle's. A change in the liquid requirements, a bow to the season, had them huddled at the bar over hot toddies.

"Man, I detest this lousy weather, not fit for man or beast," grumbled DeShales. He sipped his hot drink. "Or even Democrats." Tom was a stout Republican.

"It's the holy season. Let's leave politics out of this. And are the Democrats man or beast?"

"Definitely."

Zack grinned. A so-called independent, he usually voted a mixed ticket. No principles, Tom always said. No one, no party makes me walk in lock step, was Zack's parry. All parties are equally inept, shady, self centered. And so on, just conversation, they had worked this field, half in jest, for years.

"Anyway," said Zack, "people who bitch about the weather give me a real pain in my Fruit Of The Loom."

"How so?"

"You don't like northern weather, your privilege. Go live some place different. Then bellyache about earthquakes, hurricanes, boll weevils, whatever!"

"Lot in what you say. But if I have to give up my right to bitch about Minnesota just because I live in Minnesota don't seem right. Like, say I lived in South Florida, might like it. But if a big croc chewed off my left leg, I think I'd complain."

"How did crocs get into this?"

"They didn't really. I'm just making a point. That's what lawyers do."

"Yeah. Lawyers are a strange breed."

They gave full appreciation in their glances to a striking brunette who eased into a nearby booth. Moments later a handsome, well built man appeared and joined her. Interest waned.

"Weather be damned," said Zack. "Let her blow, let her snow, no problems."

"You have the infectious manner and vocal inflections of a happy man."

"Got that right, Webster."

"Progress on the Cassandra front?"

"You make it sound like my reports are bulletins. Dispatches from the front."

"All law is a battle. Take no prisoners."

"I didn't."

"Past tense? What gives?"

"My friend," said Zack, "justice and righteousness have prevailed."

"Last I heard you were headed for Court."

"We got to Court, yeah, we mounted those big stone steps."

"An exciting trip."

"And here's what happened, still pinching myself. Even before open arguments, Miller, that's the head mouth of the opposition, asked for a sidebar, then a conference in Chambers."

"And you, Zack, the tiger sensing fear, fear you could smell as the jungle cats do, pounced."

"Sort of. With mild disinterest. My preference was for the trial to get underway."

"Which was bullshit."

"You'll never know, Tom, the feeling that flooded over me. Had to be contained. I felt like the G.I.'s must have felt when the news flashed on VE Day. I damn near cheered, but I choked it back."

"They wanted out?"

"So bad, I think they could taste it. And I, the reluctant warrior, showed mercy."

DeShales could only shake his head. "You crazy son of a bitch."

"Part of the game. You'd have had the same feeling, same strategy."

"So, they caved?"

"Like a sand castle on a Mexican beach. They got caught in the undertow. Am I mixing metaphors here?"

DeShales motioned for refills. The toddies were potent, perhaps two were enough.

"You hold firm on the three?"

"Nope."

"What then?"

"I had never really advanced the number. Only to you – and Cassandra. Strategic reserve, you understand."

"So?" The information flow was like pulling teeth.

"All settled, signed for and delivered, without the help of FedEx. Would you believe three point six?"

"My God!"

"And mine, I hope. Someone looking out for us. And what a circus! You think you get engulfed in paper work, your line of work."

"I can imagine."

"Thirty pages, thirty single-spaced on releases alone. Cassandra had to sign at least a dozen, all in the most contrived legalese on earth. Thought I had seen something before with Boles. That was nothing compared to this. But in the end... "

"In the end the check was cut?"

"To the penny. Result, two point four to the injured lady, plus all medical and shrink bills, now and continuing. And one point two for your wealthy friend."

"Former friend."

"Say what?"

"In my practice I don't get to knock knees with wealthy barristers. You'll drop me like a good looking gal with rampaging V.D. Nice to look at, like me, but hardly worth the risk."

"Which way would you like your butt kicked?"

"The proposition, whether intended sexually or punitively, does not enthrall me."

Zack laughed. He had not felt so euphoric in years. He was, on just two drinks, near to drunkenness, the belly wrenching intensity of the past weeks lifted. He felt a tremendous release as though a parachute, stuck in free fall for moments, had miraculously opened, just a thousand feet above the ground. To be here in this place, to be financially solvent and to share good fortune with the same person with whom he had shared, so often, despair and defeat... it was a feeling beyond any he had known since law school.

DeShales shared his buddy's joy. Celebrations were in order. Shirl would have to overlook his failings for once, this was monumental. He ordered a third round and, in a steaming haze of holiday cheer, the two men belted them down. An air of unreality was abroad in the atmosphere of rich carpet and dark wood paneled walls, hung with reproductions of art to appeal to the taste for nostalgia.

And yet. And yet, Tom DeShales was struck with the same sense of justice askew that had haunted him for months. Shirl's friend had booked a feeling of something unspoken, unidentifiable but out of sync. The image had remained. Time for one more probe into an area he should avoid.

He tried an oblique approach.

"Zack, I'm so damned pleased. I just can't express my happiness."

"Thanks, Compadre."

"And my honest to God admiration for the skill and determination you've shown. Not just on this case but also on Boles."

"My job pal. That's what I do."

"Sure." DeShales loved the guy and was, for the

moment, in love with their noble profession. "All's well that ends."

"Everything does, sooner or later."

"Is there anything you'd like to tell me, Zack?"

"Beyond let's get smashed?"

"No. That's a given today. I mean about the airport rumble or the Boles case. Or, may I remove my shoes before treading on holy ground, Cassandra Janes?"

Zack laughed again. The powerful drinks were grabbing. And he didn't really give a damn, not about anything, not now.

"I can't insult you, buddy, with bullshit, you don't deserve that. And, of course, I don't really know, not positive, but you're asking for my best shot, opinion-wise, right?"

"I guess."

Zack measured his words carefully, doling them out in precise droplets. "Cassandra Janes, carefully, deliberately, with malice aforethought and felonious intention, screwed the system."

Zack paused. "What does that make me, a witting or unwitting accomplice?"

DeShales pondered, "I'd say unwitting."

"Why?"

"Because, seems to me you were far into this strange event before the doubts crept in. Then there was no backing out. Hell of a quandary for you, buddy. A duty to the system, a duty to your client."

"You've nailed it. And never easy."

"What happens now?"

Zack stared squarely at his friend. "Nothing happens. Life goes on. I deposit my check; Cassandra, I presume, does the same. The case is closed." Zack's face was a mask, the discipline in place. "Case closed," he muttered again, "there has to be closure, like a death or a divorce, legal cases end, new ones replace them."

"I'm struggling myself. But don't sweat the motives or the hidden complications. Because there may be none.

I've dealt with a person I've gotten to know and like; yet she remains a stranger. The woman hired me; I was a laborer worthy of his hire. You asked me a question, I gave you my best response, one that may have been on the money or dead wrong."

"Either way," admired DeShales, "you are one hell of a lawyer."

"And either way, we remember the drill, not just from our profession, but back to law school, the university, all our schooling." Zack Taylor studied his drink, he was deep into a sort of reverie. "Goes way back as I see it. Beyond you and I, back to the fundamentals of English common law, those attributes that distinguish us from the fascists, from dictatorship of condemnations simply because you have a government power to convict."

"You're waxing eloquent, my friend."

Zack might not have heard. "In our system, mistakes can be made, frequently are made. But the drill remains. If guilty persons cannot be represented, who will be there to represent the innocent?"

While the two attorneys contemplated the intricacies of legality, morality and reality over hot toddies in the elegance of Crestburg's most traditional restaurant and lounge, Galen and Cassandra Janes relaxed over coffee and homemade peanut butter cookies at the kitchen table of their house. The scene of loving domesticity might have appeared to an outside observer a contradiction to a sudden accumulation of wealth, a windfall engineered and executed flawlessly, a demonstration of the rewards of crime. But there could be no outside observer; the crimes had been so perfectly carried out that all people who were aware of the facts felt, not only no condemnation of Cassandra but, only concern and sympathy for the injuries she had sustained. So, with her husband of twenty seven years, she basked in the satisfaction of recompense for crimes that were, in her mind, not crimes at all, merely the hand of justice at work, a strike for egalitarianism and a matter of finally making the odds more even for the less fortunate. The bulging coffers of the super rich do not spring a leak voluntarily, the fissure must be encouraged by intelligent action. And so on.

Galen, sharing none of her views, knew the sharp pangs of conscience. He was truly troubled, shaken by knowledge that put his sense of guilt, his feeling for humanity, at odds with the happiness of his wife. Life, thought Galen, is a masterwork of conflicts. This was one where the outcome was ordained. He would never, never betray his wife or harp on actions that were intolerable to most of his peers and neighbors. The deal is done, the check is cashed and invested, let the water close over where the body was dropped.

Cass, carefree, insouciant, knew something of the conflicts that bothered her husband and was, for that reason, the more grateful for his unwavering support. Had his intellect and ideals matched hers, it would have been easy. The vast gulf of morality between them could not be obliterated but Galen, through Herculean effort, had made the adjustment, not soul deep, but on the surface. Will Galen learn to enjoy the security he deserves? I truly believe he will, she thought. If not, in the years ahead, he may wish to funnel back to society whatever he thought society merited, to balance the books. We all live with our demons; Gale, who has lived for more than twenty-five years on borrowed time, could possess worse demons, and perhaps did possess them, from the old horrors of the Asian peninsula and a war that could not be won because his country faltered when the chips were down.

"In a trance, hon?" she asked. "You seem miles away. You're invited back."

"I do tend to glaze over at times," Galen murmured. "In the worst times in Nam, my buddies called me a dreamer. Actually, I was so certain I would never survive that I sometimes lost interest in a life and a world I wouldn't live to experience. And, you remember, when

Andy was caught up in that whirlwind of addiction, I just about gave up in utter despair."

"Could've fooled me, hon. You handled the situation better than any Dad in the world could have. You were wonderful, as I recall." Cassandra smiled, remembering. "Those were the days that cemented this family together. Tough times. We survived them. And you were untouchable, they couldn't lay a glove on you."

"Oh hell, dumb luck. And you helped me more than I appreciated at the time. Now, I'm on your team for the duration."

"That's right, you've got the contract. Don't you ever try to break it."

"No chance. You'd have Zack Taylor on my ass before I knew what hit me!"

The Criminal Housewife

CHAPTER 21

A pledge of secrecy, of protecting anonymity, is easy to make, often impossible, given the vagaries of human nature, for most people to honor, no matter how diligently one tries. Friendships have been shattered, divorces granted, even duels fought, thriving businesses brought down by secrets kept, secrets betrayed. Madge Evans was privy to information that she had no right to possess.

And in this December night, three days before Christmas, when the unleashed power of windswept fury in northern latitudes swept through the city of Crestburg, she considered the recent events that her employer had revealed to her, revealed in the comforting arena of bedroom intimacy, that erogenous zone of pillow talk, whisperings and sharing.

On this bitter night Madge had worked late, a common practice for the devoted secretary, then locked up and enjoyed – tolerated – a solitary meal at Ching's, Crestburg's oldest and best Chinese restaurant. She loved to eat, her solitary life since her mid-twenties divorce demanded bodily comfort but serious overweight, with all the attendant side effects, both physical and mental, horrified her. Madge had a tough routine of stretching and exercising, thousands of miles had been logged on her bikes, both outdoor and stationary and she ate those wonderful foods that satisfied with the low calories of noodles and watercress. Hot tea and a fortune cookie were added, the paper slip within the delicacy reading: "You are an honorable person and deserve great happiness." What a crock of pseudo-eastern stargazing, she thought. It might all be true, but how did the cookie baker know that this honorable gal would be so reassured?

My life is such a mess that no Chinese soothsayer could find a solution for me at this stage. So I'll just have to figure it out for myself. Some assignment! That vicious, claw fingered Shirl is the pothole in the road. I have to get around her somehow, without damaging the undercarriage. If only Tom knew I harbored such thoughts, what would he say? I think – I think he would say "you're right, darling, that pothole has stripped my gears for over twenty years. That obstruction should be removed."

Madge manufactured herself a drink, a martini as cool and calculating as any bar professional could muster. Between her secret and rigidly controlled boozing and her vibrant fantasies of Tom DeShales in her arms and in her bed, Madge led, as do many other women – and men – a life within a life, years of reaching out with her mind and, until recently, holding back with her body, that encompassed her existence. I can't get it on with any other guy, not that the pickings are that attractive or available. When quiet desire becomes raging obsession, all bets are off. He said he would call tonight by eleven. How many promises broken, how many hopes dissolved in the cold?

The loyal secretary loved her apartment, actually a condo, in a middle class area, with wonderful, understanding neighbors and amenities of pool and tennis court. Should things ever work out for her, she would hate to leave. She had acquired, at thirty-five, a mid-life comfortableness in her home. Madge had always been a legal secretary with two previous employers before her liaison with DeShales. The rotund attorney, with his braggadocio and sloppy mannerisms had turned her off. But only for a few months. Gradually, she became fond of his indulgent ways and near maternal about his cloying dependence and love/hate relationship upon a wife Madge had met only twice. The first encounter had been cautious; the second almost more than Madge's hostility could contain. But contain she did and remained little more than furniture to Shirl.

At eleven-thirty the phone rang. Madge shivered as she answered. Why, she wondered, at this stage, is casualness far beyond me?

"That you, baby?" Madge was happy the husky voice carried no hint of alcohol, the old desire to be something more than an island retreat for a man in his cups.

"No, it's Brooke Shields, you son of a bitch. Madge left when you didn't call at eleven."

"Brookie, baby, how's it going? Six feet of buxom beauty, as I recall."

They laughed together in that special way of a man and a woman who share the humor of conspiracy.

"Anyway, it's late," she yawned deliciously. "You coming over?"

"Can't tonight. No chance."

"Lock down from the warden?"

"What warden? I'm a free spirit. No one yanks my chain."

"Yeah, right."

Now Tom DeShales purred. "There'll be other times, babe. Let's not quarrel."

"You're right. I'm sorry." Madge detested herself for that statement, impossible to hold back.

"Here's something might interest you."

"Shirl is knocked up?"

"If she is, I am definitely not guilty." Tom slipped into his lawyerly mode. "For such a calamity to occur, there must exist intent, opportunity and completed action. I plead innocent."

"I know all about your innocence, boss."

He was hurt. "I'm never your boss when the office is closed. Just an ardent admirer."

"That's sweet. What might interest me?"

There was a long silence. Has he been detected by Shirl, or something electronic, she wondered. "Tom?"

"Yeah, well it's like this. I haven't played straight with my buddy, Zack. Spilled all the beans to you, remember?"

"Sure. You regret it now?"

"Nah. I think we're entitled to share everything. Makes us closer, way I figure." She could almost see him squirming. He really is a dear man, things bother him.

"Tom, we've gone over this. If I'm not trustworthy on anything you tell me, we haven't got much going."

"Yeah, yeah, sure. But the bigness is, I just can't keep it in, Zack won his case."

"The big one with the local blonde?"

"The same. Tipped on her ass in the Twin Cities Airport by a shuttle cart."

"Flying low, huh?"

"You might say. Big negotiations for weeks, yammer, yammer, you know how it goes. Zack was petrified of going to court. Put on a show, of course, but really scared, I believe."

"What happened?"

"Bluffed it through. Settled and sealed out of court. And you won't believe the amount!"

Madge snorted, she wouldn't be talked down to by anyone, even Tom.

"Judas, Mr. DeShales, I've been around you or various legal hacks – sorry, you're excluded – for a dozen years. What in hell would surprise me?"

"How about three point six mil?"

Madge, like her boss before, was truly impressed. She sipped the last of her second martini.

"Wow! That does knock my socks off. That's way beyond anything I've been exposed to." She was tender now, shared moments, her weakness. "Will this be on the news or in the local paper?"

"Don't think so. Or any news media, near as I know.

The big boys don't want precedents aired that will come back to haunt them."

"What about her, Mrs. Janes, isn't it?"

"I assume she had to sign some non-disclosure agreement. She may or may not honor such a deal. Once the check is cashed, they'd play hell getting any of it back. Money doesn't flow both ways."

"Sure as heck doesn't flow my way."

"Would you like a list of the legal secs in this town that get far less than you? You are pampered, petted, adored and overpaid, sweetheart."

"Nice speech, Simon. And where would you get this list? Your lawyer buddies would lie just as much as you, con man." Madge laughed. "Besides, I have hidden assets."

"Not that well hidden."

"Hidden from guys who hide behind their wives' skirts, stranger."

The conversation, inane as it was, dwindled from that point and signed off with resounding busses over the wire. Madge thought, I never did actually determine if he called from home or, more likely, some watering hole. Well, what the hell.

Madge viewed again, with martini in hand, the broken pieces of her life. This is a tangled mess that wouldn't ever pass muster on the soaps, she muttered. Why have I gotten my sweet self into this?

She knew the answers. One was proximity, the constant physical nearness of a man with a lethal combination of virtue and vices, a man swift to anger, swift to forgive. DeShales' recurring status as pigeon and cuckold had, through the years, aroused in her a fierce protectiveness. Why is this good man being hurt when so many men, near to evil, were adored and catered to by the women in their lives? She could, by no stretch of the imagination, consider herself a home wrecker. What in the world was there to wreck in a marriage that contained as one partner a grasping hellion with calluses on her backside. Shirl's sporadic attempts at reform and reconciliation infuriated the secretary even more than her – alleged – unfaithfulness.

This man, Tom DeShales, is a treasure. And one fine day – not just an occasional stolen hour – I will surely possess him for good. Madge raised her glass, near empty. "Here's to you, Shirl, you bitch of the world. Your day in the dunk tub is on its way."

She paused to consider. "Or, maybe not. That strange and possibly crooked Zack Taylor evades the judge's bench. Maybe our situation will luck out as well."

"I don't want to see my darling dragged through a messy divorce action if it ever comes to that. Going down that road is rough and the repercussions can be devastating. I've been around this law business long enough to know that Shirl would surely dredge up some piranhic barrister who could cut Tom to shreds, fiscally and emotionally."

"Ah, hell, he – we – could handle it. And the net result might be wonderful if – what a huge if – it ever happens."

Chapter 22

Christmas Day at the Janes' household did not follow the pattern set by many previous years. "Old habits are made to be broken," announced Cassandra. "I work like a slave the night before, fix the turkey and trimmings, then the next morning to church and, afterwards, good old Mom back to the kitchen."

"Your own fault," Galen winked at Andy. "World's best cook, voted by a landslide. What do you expect?"

"Best cook – you bet. I've burned my share of handsome birds in my day and the damn mashed potatoes always had lumps like golf balls. It's all over, folks. A lot of terrific establishments in this town, even on a holiday. They need the business, I don't. You guys pay terrible and tip like barrio landlords." She grinned. "I won't say the Janes' kitchen is closed for the duration. I can still knock out a grilled cheese without breaking a sweat. And cold cereal. I'm all American on those little nuggets."

"But, starting today, we run up the tab at some other place, is that it?" Meg was secretly delighted, considering herself put upon as cook's helper. "Well, some places are closed today, how about the Hyatt Hotel – a cinch they'll be trolling for customers."

"Sounds great, hon."

"Sounds like an arm and a leg to me," demurred Galen, the shackles of a cost deprived lifetime hard to break. "Hotel food is okay, but aimed at the well-heeled tourists and clinic patients."

Cass laughed. She could not fully adjust herself to their present conditions. She held out her arm, almost completely mended, no scars apparent. "I'm a medical casualty, in excruciating pain and discomfort. Broken in mind and body, in need of sustenance."

"Well, that does it," said Andy. "One out of four on morning sick call. The healthy and hardy among us will have to make allowances. We were brought up, weren't we, Meg, to help the elderly and infirm."

And so they proceeded to the Hyatt for their Christmas dinner, a splendid meal. "I'm buying," said Cassandra. "And I'm in no mood, though merry and holy the season, to listen to any shit about it."

"Son of a gun," muttered Andy. "Outfumbled again. Oh well, a hundred bucks here and there. I'm still at a loss on all this. Been checking the lottery winners. Can't find a name I know."

Cass ignored the smart mouth remarks. The family feasted on the Hyatt holiday special, a smorgasbord of turkey, ham, mountains of fresh fruit, vegetables and salad fixings without end. Cassandra and Galen could hardly contain their happiness; there had not been this much real togetherness in a long time. Thought the actor, Galen, I've much thinking and planning for the future to face in the coming months. That's my problem and the implications of that problem sear my soul. All in its proper time, which certainly isn't today.

The family drove home in a lazy roundabout way, admiring the pure whiteness of the winter beauty on the outskirts of town and into the farm country. This country of agricultural splendor, industrial wealth and medical dominance constituted all the hearth and home the Janes family had been born into. Problems of Andy's troubled youth and Meg's fierce loyalty to the disadvantaged dissolved in togetherness as they traveled terrain where Galen had bagged rabbits, squirrels and, in season, a few corn-fed deer.

Many people who live in this area do not hold in their hearts a true thankfulness for the beauty and energy of the Upper Midwest, thought Galen. When I was in 'Nam, suffocated by heat and humidity, even on the open rice paddies, I could only remember the wonders of the changing seasons back home. And, in the jungle, that house of green horrors that concealed death at every turn of the trail, the depression I suffered was another kind of wounding. Not the purple heart of blood and battered flesh, but the mind-bending torture of breathless enfoldment. Every rustle, every bird song – was it real or feigned by the invisible enemy? We never knew for sure, but guys on point were found with their throats slit, soundless slaughter when we had never heard a sound that might be human.

Somehow, twenty odd years later, I still cannot figure how I survived when so many did not, names on a black wall in Washington, D.C. Oh, hell, holidays do this to me.

Back at the old house, They exchanged presents, an old custom in their home of gift giving late on Christmas Day. The gifts to the "children" were far more lavish than in years past, expensive clothing from Boles and top retailers in the Twin Cities. The kids were stunned by the presents. In addition to the top brand clothing, there was a new 19-inch color TV for Andy and a five hundred dollar gift certificate – Dayton's – for Meg.

Andy and Meg raised eyebrows at each other – new strands were continually unfolding in the mysteries surrounding their mother's reticence. Galen examined his impressive new lathe equipment for his workshop. Cass crooned over a gold necklace and new perfumes and lotions. In the bathroom she caressed her arms and shoulders with imported oils and admired the near perfection of the battered arm. "What a piece of work," she murmured. "In a lifetime of getting booted around and harassed by bill collectors, how did I ever luck into such medical perfection?" She examined more closely. "The broken wing of the sparrow has been restored. I can soar. With Galen I <u>will</u> soar and let the devil take the hindmost." She grinned at remembrance of the old bromides, thumb to the nose challenges she had learned in childhood from an alcoholic and improvident father.

Her mother was a dim and distraught memory who had quietly faded away in Cassandra's early childhood.

The mind plays tricks and Cassandra could find no exception to that syndrome. Here it is, the Christmas season, the very day, in fact. I'm rolling in dough, fraudulently acquired, and the doubts and implications of guilt gnaw at my edges. Let them gnaw! I put those feelings behind me many months back when I embarked on this uncharted flight. If there is some disharmony in my spirit from what I've accomplished, small price to pay for tipping the balance, for bringing the bubble into its calibrated niche in the cosmic level.

The poor rob from the wealthy and it's a crime. The rich rob from the rest of us and it's just the proper operation of the capitalist system. They feel no remorse because they are insulated in the warm complacency of their rightful place in the upper echelons of a stratified society. If they – and "they" consists of more people than I can imagine – are immune to the end results of their beliefs, then screw them, so am I. My radicalism has never died, even though it has often wavered.

Render unto Caesar – right on. They'd have to cut this arm off, not just injure it, before I'd return a red cent. And, in any event, the attorneys, on both sides, made out like bandits. What's new?

Over popcorn and apple cider the nuclear family was immersed in a sense of contentment. Too much peace. Meg could not hold back.

"So, Mom, I figure we're high on the hog, as Grampa used to say, because of your accident. Are you going to tell your loving daughter and son just how much money was involved?"

"No.

"Why not?"

"Because it's not the time."

"Great answer, Mom," said Meg. In another easy chair, a worn recliner, Galen observed this with feigned indifference.

Cassandra sighed.

"You guys. I should be mad but I'm not. There's some explaining due to the family. I'll go along with that. But listen up and carefully; this special bulletin may not be repeated." Cassandra drew a deep breath. "Pass the damn popcorn, Andy. Ever hear of share and share alike?"

"You talking about these old maids left in the bowl or the angelic folks in Minneapolis?"

Cass laughed. "Well, there's been a wee bit of sharing from that direction. Yes, the holiday season overcame the dear people."

"But – you didn't read in the paper about the case. The TV was blacked out. There's an agreement, signed and sealed to protect all parties. What would you call that, Mr. Attorney?"

"I'm not sure. Something along the line of confidential settlement, all parties protected, now and in the future – all papers sealed."

Galen permitted himself a small smile.

"You got it," said Cassandra. "Both parties protected, even family members. I had about decided not to tell you two any of the details. Now, thank the Lord, it's been taken out of my hands, not without breaking the iron bonds that bind me."

"What a conniver you are," marveled Andy. "You really wanted an out to stifle our adolescent curiosity. And, wham – they provided you with the perfect document. Gilt-edged and, I presume, dripping with legalese."

"You didn't think, did you, that you were the only sharp barrister in the world?"

Meg squealed in delight. "What a runaround, bro. We're both left gasping for air like a couple of fish in a hamper." She implored her mother. "But couldn't you drop a few hints and stay out of jail?"

"Jail talk gives me the shivers." Cassandra gazed at her kids proudly. "No, not a word, and, in your shoes, I'd feel the same as you do. But, hey, grab this. It's more than a little and less than a lot. That should be a cinch for a couple of brilliant brains to unravel. Like breaking the Japanese code after Pearl Harbor."

The best of the popcorn had been polished off, the cider bottle nearly empty.

"And I have a fight to pick with you, Andrew. Might as well be on Christmas."

"Yeah? As if I didn't know."

"I advanced you some cash to get back on the academic track, if you recall, by cutting back on off-campus work. And you haven't lived up to your word."

"I know." Andy was guilty. "This sounds dumb but I'd like to specialize in industrial law. So, I've been keeping my hand in, looking ahead."

"Looking for a breakdown, you mean."

"You're right, Mom. I'll be cutting back real soon. I just – I just somehow felt the thirty big ones were unreal. Like I'd wake up, busted again." Andy was tortured from the deceit. But his inborn cautiousness, a strange trait forged in the furnace of his teenage wildness, had sounded a voice in his brain that said "this can't be true, it's just too pat, too perfect for reality." And so he had played it cool, close to the vest, to see what followed.

"I've been a skeptic, Mom. That's just me. If Publishers Sweepstakes came to me with a million bucks, I'd be positive they had the wrong address."

"Get over it."

"Yeah, shape up," offered Meg. "I've only got one brother, a sorry specimen, but better than none, I guess."

"Don't try my patience, squirt. I can still paddle the crap out of you."

"Fat chance. You're so skinny I'd wipe the floor with you. I'm tougher than roofing nails."

"And just as flat headed."

The brother and sister took off for the movies. The parents did not inquire the name or suitability of the film. Those days were long gone and had really made little difference in the past. Galen and Cassandra relaxed in the warm embrace of the old living room. Memories flooded back at this time of year, this crossroads in the journey of their married life.

Galen smiled.

"Well," he said, "you did it again, hon. The Con Woman of the Year had spin control they could use along the Potomac."

"Say which?"

"I'll give you 'say which.' This bullshit about the agreement. Where'd that fiction come from?"

"Gale, I had to think fast. Did the best I could, but I was floundering. Couldn't you tell?"

"Naw. You're light on your feet, a counter puncher."

She was tired.

"Some day – some day. Gale, we all use that old chestnut. But it's too much to lay on them at one time. The kids might choke on it."

"Not likely."

"Let the transition be just a bit more gradual, that's all I ask. We've got years ahead to work it out."

"I guess."

"If they think a couple hundred of the big bills were all that came down, it's what? Better for their emotional health, their personalities."

"I'm inclined to agree."

"Thanks for that."

"I'm not good with words but you've come close enough as I see it."

"They'll know some day, Gale. There's a time, a season for everything. Even sex."

"Now that you mention it."

The Criminal Housewife

CHAPTER 23

Domestic bliss at the DeShales house had, once again, began to pall. Tom DeShales, a bit slimmer and trimmer, felt he had done his part to patch things up. Drinking was curtailed, if far from eliminated, gambling was still an outlet, but he had managed to knock off the long dialogues when the game ended and drove home at a decent hour, just beyond midnight. DeShales, always the long-suffering man, exaggerated his contribution to the marriage vows.

I've turned into a plaster saint, he muttered to himself. I oughta be riding on somebody's dashboard, an inspiration to the sacred institution of legal bondage. What the hell does the woman want? She was great for a while. Now she's turning into a witch again. And using those new wheels that I'm still making payments on to jounce around who the hell knows where. To her girl friends, of course, oldest dodge in the world. And who are her main pals – old gals with tinted hair and hollow legs. Divorced and on the make, they chase guys like Zack Taylor and I chase game. Game, that's the word, it's all a game to them. DeShales conveniently forgot his past admiration for most of the ladies involved. Solid, attractive women from the Country Club, they loomed now, in imagination, as harridans... all, save for the lovely Madge Evans.

A man comes into this tough world a bachelor. That must be the natural state of things. Marriage is a contrived, legalistic arrangement, ostensibly to establish family, but actually to bring discipline and compliance to males, imprisonment while the jailers continue on their merry way. I'm beginning to reach a plateau of incoherence, he thought, I'm getting out of hand with my brooding. Last summer these matters drove me a little crazy, to the point of actually spying. But never again, the flicker isn't worth the candle. He pulled his Bronco into the East Side Tavern lot and sauntered in to meet again with Zack Taylor.

Ah, the friendship, the camaraderie of men. Women have never understood it, never will. We don't ask for perfection in our pals, in fact, we would be embarrassed to be tight with a guy who was obviously better than ourselves. Where would we find a level of comfort?

We prefer the openness of the flawed, no matter if that includes a weakness for drink, profanity, insecurity, a larcenous nature or any other breach in the human dike that separates the civil from the denizens of the urban jungle.

On Groundhog Day the weather was vile, typical February. Cold, windy, with a moderate snowfall adding to the eighteen inches already on the ground. Far from Crestburg, Minnesota, in Pennsylvania, a small brown animal peeped out at the world, and news of his sight lines, did he or did he not observe his shadow, became the grist of news organizations with little else to do. Said Tom DeShales, "why the hell don't they get a life?"

"You mean," said Zack Taylor, "like yours?"

"I've got a life. I am a successful, though struggling, attorney, a devout church member. I roar with the local Lions and fly with the Eagles." DeShales considered his hollow days. "Not to mention American Legion and a stalwart member of the Arts Council."

"Truly a Renaissance man, Mr. DeShales, a man for all ages."

"Nice to be so recognized. And Lord knows, I'm feeling my age. Pushing forty-eight is like pushing that rock uphill we're always reading about. Keeps coming back at you."

"Does it ever. That mother-loving rock!"

A change of pace, the two legal warriors had a go at gin and tonic. A civilized drink, avowed DeShales, the off-Broadway bar quiet in the late afternoon.

"How's business, Zack?"

"Slow. In a change of pace, I'm representing a mad wife. Not really mad, but battered. Her story is solid, long history with an asshole husband. Black eye, loosened teeth, you know the picture."

"Sure. Does it ever change? And is there any money available?"

"Not enough to matter. Damn close to a charity case for me. But I've known the woman for years, she actually helped take care of Billy for a time. Wonderful gal, so I owe her, she just got dealt a bad hand. The son of a bitch involved makes good money. I think auto parts. But it'll be tough to get a piece of it, no matter what the court rules."

"Yeah. Well, sounds interesting."

"Sort of, with the personal friendship involved. But since last fall, I'm spoiled for other cases."

"After Cassandra, the earth is a bleached and barren planet, I assume."

"Correct, not nearly as exciting. And not nearly as remunerative. A guy like me, like you, gets one great case in a lifetime. Mine was the fair Cassandra, mystery woman of the decade. Haven't really figured her out to this day."

"Oh, I think you have."

"Yeah? You could be wrong, buddy. And I know what you're getting at."

"And, conversely, I could be right." DeShales grinned. "Right, wrong, or a little of each."

"Or this and that. Hell, we rolled all those possibilities around in December. We didn't know for sure then, we don't now."

"It's just, the whole thing seemed too pat, too good to

be true."

"I'll admit there's an incomprehensible element. Forever unknown. But I've put it to bed."

"That's her husband's job," DeShales rolled his eyes, "and very nice work, I imagine."

"Imagination is as far as I got. The woman is true blue near as I know. The nearest I ever came to a flirtatious mode was to suggest, playfully, that inside that iron exterior was, perhaps, a wild woman trying to escape. Cassandra just laughed, in that saucy way of hers, and said I could be right but she was determined to keep that wild woman imprisoned. Jail breaks just lead to other problems."

"Out of the mouths of babes. Some babe."

"The money beat the hell out of rumpus room action though it might have been nice to have both."

"What are they doing with that truck load of dough?"

"Not a great deal yet but Cassandra says they have big plans. Galen still goes to work every day, but in a new car. They bought stuff for the kids, I guess, and they plan a big trip to Europe in the spring, Galen says if he can get off work. Cassandra says, if he can't get off, screw the hardware store, go anyway."

"That's what I'd do. I mean what's that dinky-ass job compared to a trip of a lifetime? None of us have that much time. And don't let me get started on mortality issues today. What a washout I'd've been as the Reverend my Mom hoped for in the flush of my brilliant youth!" DeShales ordered another round of drinks. "Anything new with your boy?"

The old refrain. Zack appreciated the concern but hated the question, the answer elusive. "Naw, well maybe. The Clinic is trying some new approach, supposed to be a great breakthrough. Seems like it helps, but maybe I'm just hoping." Zack Taylor studied his fresh drink. "I'll always keep hoping, I can't ever accept that autism is that unbreakable. But, maybe it is, in the end, one of those afflictions that's out of reach."

"He have a good Christmas?"

"I guess. But how do you ever really know?"

"What a life. Strange turns. That beautiful boy of yours can't talk. My wife can't stop talking."

"Hell, you've got more wife than you deserve, you dog. Know what, you put Shirl on the market, she's gone in a flash. The woman keeps you on your best behavior because she keeps you guessing."

DeShales was in grudging agreement. "Oh, she's OK. And your wife, Jan, remains, as always, the homecoming queen."

"You got that right, friend. You don't always get things right but, on this, I can't even argue. Pity, because I can debate you under the table."

"In a horse's south end, you can."

And, sure enough, in the second month of the year, the trip of a lifetime was planned for Mr. and Mrs. Galen Janes. Plane tickets were booked for early in May.

This was an adventure to the Old Country, or rather, several countries, loosely planned and open to any and all diversions. They had rejected all the proffered package tours, the itineraries on each left out too much of their desires.

"I can't stand to be herded about like sheep on a Montana ranch," said Cassandra. "We'll just be gypsies, hon, go anywhere and everywhere. How long? Who knows, maybe two months, maybe more. If we find a town that suits us, we might stay for a week or more."

Galen agreed. Quiet and conservative though he had become, there was a fire re-ignited in his belly, a renewal of old dreams. The cold countries of the North and the languid lands of the Mediterranean, North Africa and Egypt beckoned him. An avid National Geographic reader, he had absorbed a tremendous layman's knowledge of written and pictorial background through the years. Now he wished to flesh out his plebian dreams with reality. Galen had been reluctant; now he could hardly wait and Cass was fascinated by his eagerness.

I've finally awakened this sleeping giant, she thought fondly. At five nine, not exactly a giant, but her one and only hero.

The new optimism was not confined to the parents, it was contagious to the whole family. Andy and Meg were aglow with delight for the planned journey. They would have gladly joined their parents. For some unknown reason, money seemed no object, but both realized that Mom had been injured and compensated, to what extent they had no idea.

"Forget it, Kids," said Cassandra. "Maybe another time. But this is a second honeymoon, a quarter century overdue so, for this time, butt out." There had been little protest, both kids had experienced new leases on life. In the past few months came an end to scrimping. They knew not to push.

In Minneapolis, events were shaping up in a manner to please the parents, even though Andy had procrastinated two months.

At the Acme Manufacturing Company (builders of lawn mowers and garden tools) Jim Fischer, foreman, lighted a cigarette and viewed with mild dispassion, the young man sitting across from his desk. Fischer, mild mannered, had viewed many young men, mostly U students, come and go in the past eighteen years, none better than Andy Janes.

"So, you're, cutting out, Andy?"

"No, cutting down. If you'll allow it."

"We're flexible. What you got in mind?"

"Ten, twelve hours a week."

Fischer grimaced. He had responsibility to keep the assembly lines running, check procured materials and constantly improve quality. Workers drifting in and out did not pan out and Andy was no machinist.

"Looks to me like you plan to be just a tourist around here. Stop in now and again, visit with the boys, pinch a boob on the secretaries and be on your way."

"It's not that way, Mr. Fischer."

"Jim."

"Right, Jim. It's just, my studies are going to pot."

"Pot?"

"Not that kind. I'm not keeping up. Bone tired all the time. I'm worried, Jim, my folks are worried, my girl friend. I sort of have one, but hardly ever see her except in class. She's ready to dump me and I don't blame her."

"So you need this Kindergarten schedule with us so you'll have more sack time with your pet squeeze?"

Andy laughed. He had never had a better friend than the forty-two year old veteran of the small industry wars, where sales are tough and competition fierce. Jim Fischer was a company man all the way yet friendly as a spotted puppy.

"Think about it, Jim. I've been on this thirty-five hour work schedule for close to two years. The bucks just were not there without it. Now, things are different."

"Different how?"

"I can make it without the long hours. Could even scratch through with no outside job. But I like it here. Maybe some day when I'm a lawyer I can do some legal work for the company."

"At the same hourly rate I'm paying you now?"

"Well, close."

Jim Fischer laughed. "Sure. Eight bucks an hour, one hundred bucks an hour. I can credit your ambition, Andy. We'd all like a license to steal."

"See what I'll have to put up with when the time comes. Smartass lawyer jokes."

"And already you can't handle them." But the foreman had empathy for the younger man, thinking perhaps of two teenagers at home.

"What can you give us?"

"Twelve hours a week, max. Prefer ten if you could work it out."

"I wish you weren't such a good worker, Andy, I'd kick you right out of the office." Fischer worked over his time sheets and schedules. "Yeah, I can give you the hours Mondays and Tuesdays. Lots of absentees after lost weekends."

"Wonderful."

"Where the hell did you get the money, you're so flush, so independent, all of a sudden. Rob a bank?"

"Actually, yes. But just a small one."

And so the deal, the verbal contract, if it could be so called, was affirmed between Acme and Fischer's favorite student. Andy left the office more at peace than at any time he could remember. To keep your hand in the working world was great, a balance wheel in his existence. He carried the confidence of thirty thousand in the bank, an amount that secured his future, through graduation and the beginning of law school. Andy had no idea of the fortune that his mother's airport injury had gained for the family. He knew only of a freak accident on a concourse, a broken arm, now as sound as ever, and a journey planned to far away places for Mom and Dad.

CHAPTER 24

And so the long awaited journey began. On a north/south plan, they flew first to Denmark. They delighted for days in the ambience of that intriguing nation of old farms and modern cities. Then to Norway and Sweden, not just the cosmopolitan southern areas, but all the way, by train, to the northern tip, where the long, lazy days stretched near to midnight before the brief darkness crept in. Tired sleep was followed by three a.m. mornings. Cassandra and Galen could not cram enough hours into their sojourn to the north. Stockholm and other towns followed. Cass shopped for Nordic treasures to send back home. Next, they ferried across the Gulf of Bothnia to spend three fascinating days in Finland.

Amazing, they agreed. But our adventure has only just begun. Next came the wonders and historical monuments of Central Europe, the Slavic nations, Germany and France. They went first to Budapest and, after days of exploring that ancient capital, the Queen of the Danube, booked passage on a river vessel to explore that fabled river through Hungary and Austria to Passau. "We have discovered the beating heart of old Europe," marveled Cassandra. "How could we have spent our entire lives in a cocoon of ignorance about all this beauty and history?" Galen quietly agreed but refrained from such exuberance.

Days were spent in the wondrous city of Vienna. Concerts and musical festivals of all kinds delighted the travelers and, like a fairy tale come true, a ride on the Riesenrod, the one hundred year old giant Ferris Wheel seen in 'The Third Man' and other movies. A visit to Emperor Franz Joseph's ornate Opera House and meals at the Grinzing Wine Village. High as two wind swept kites, they reveled in the glow that would not diminish.

Then they rejoined the river cruise on another vessel. The days and nights turned into a mosaic of names that had only been known to them from books and films. Kelheim, Nurnberg, Hassfurt, Wurzburg. Then the end of the line, through Heidelberg to Mainz and another river cruise, this one on the Rhine. They explored Koblenz, tasted the sweet wines of Cologne, and into the low countries all the way to Amsterdam, brains swirling from all they had seen and felt in the wonderful river voyages.

"Can any woman who lives and breathes explore this part of the world and not visit Paris?" asked Cass. Galen could only agree. They rented a car and meandered through the bloody battlefields of two long ago wars, visited the Cathedral of Reims, and sent picture postcards, as they did at nearly every stop, to Andy and Meg. There was no one else, the Janes family alone in the world, only cousins, far removed, that no longer enlarged their lives.

Next came Paris and the surrounding cities. Galen marveled at the knowledge of history and culture that, somehow, Cassandra had accumulated. She tossed it off, "just bits and pieces that have stuck in my brain from all the years I longed to be here." Cass seemed designed for a wandering life and was almost indefatigable. I figured, through years of fishing and hunting, plus the racquet ball battles with Taylor, that I had remarkable stamina, thought Galen. Compared to this human dynamo, I'm a wimp! And her insatiability was evident in other aspects, the old by-the-calendar routines had been discarded. It was as though the woman was determined, driven to pack into these golden days and nights all the power and longing and sensitivity she had harnessed in the past.

And yet, at times, Cassandra wearied. She is doing too much, thought Galen, we must devise a more reasonable pace. But, after a day, full speed ahead resumed. All that could be seen must be visited and absorbed, as though the hands of the clock were an unrelenting taskmaster.

Greece and the magic islands of the Aegean followed their time in France. The weather, warming into full summer, brought days of intense heat. We did all this backwards, they humorously agreed; we should have booked south to north instead of the other way. But, what the hell, we'll bronze our bodies in this glorious sunshine, heavy sunblock lotion will hold the sunburn to a minimum. They traveled to Turkey and were spellbound by the ancient wonders in Ankara, Cappadocia and Hierapolis.

In the most renowned city, by beauty and history, they spent nearly a week in Istanbul, crossroad to the mysteries of Asia.

The spice bazaar and the colorful covered bazaar displayed wonders they had never witnessed and all merchandise for sale. Cassandra bought gifts for the kids, delighting in the haggling over gold and copper pieces, remembrances that Andy and Meg would treasure. Then back to Athens for a time, exploring the fabled ruins, before departing for the adventures and dangers of the land of the Pharaohs.

The soul enriching experience of the Great Pyramids and the excavated Sphinx were visited first. At Cassandra's insistence, they both mounted grouchy camels, at exorbitant prices, and dutifully purchased the pictures, proof of our damn foolishness, muttered Galen, in good nature. He knew they would find future pleasure in these and other mementoes of the journey. They took a boat trip up the Nile, not the entire distance to the Aswan Dam, but to Luxor and the Valley of the Kings and the tomb of Tutankhamen. Then back to Cairo and more days and nights in the city that stands poised in the doorway of the beginnings of modern civilization. Cairo, now a metropolis of exotic experience and certain dangers, was even greater than they had expected.

More adventures were planned. "We'll cruise the

entire coast of Africa, stopping where we feel welcome," said Galen. First Alexandria, then eastward, bypassing Libya, to Tunisia and Morocco and even, by their culture and movie viewing, the ultimate, the fabled city of Casablanca.

It was not to be. One morning the pain in Cassandra's abdomen, something she had been unwilling to admit, that she had been forcing into submission, became too great. After a cursory examination at a Cairo clinic, they drove to the airport and boarded a flight for the United States, and from there to home. They had been away a total of forty-seven days. Meg and Andy met them at the Crestburg Airport.

By the following morning, Cassandra Janes was in a local hospital, in great discomfort and even greater frustration at this interruption in her life and plans. How could this happen to me and why this soon? In an avalanche of pain, with the near certainty of surgery and chemotherapy ahead, her mind reached out to destinations and experiences as yet unfulfilled. My itinerary is screwed up, how can I possibly abide something like this? Just for a bellyache – I can't believe a detour like this. I've beat them all, outsmarted everyone, the hotshot attorneys and investigators from Boles and the airport, the BCA, for all I know. Just an old country gal and they were all no match for the admirable Mr. Taylor and myself.

Where in all this have my aspirations disappeared to? I live and breathe and dream the bustle and breathlessness of new places, new experiences. Where in this new milieu are Spain, Portugal and glorious sunbaked Italy and the Riviera? And beyond them, my dreams carry me to dear old England, to Stonehenge, Wales and Scotland and the green fields and mountain streams of Ireland.

London, Stonehenge and Land's End were never seen by the redoubtable scam artist of the Midwest. Scotland, Wales and rain drenched Ireland remained in the future for Andy and Meg, legacy of their mother's wanderlust, handed down to her children. Unfulfilled dreams and visions, thought Galen. In every life there are many, for Cassandra, the numbers were as limitless as the fertile imagination that had financed the first exploration, the only exploration for the driven spirit.

Galen and Cassandra had returned in early July. In twelve weeks, Cassandra was dead. The technology of modern medicine had prolonged, in controlled agony, her departure but had not been successful in preventing her passing, a crossing over that was fought with all the ebbing strength at her command.

No expense was spared. Beyond the strictures of the abundant insurance, Galen haunted the Clinic and hospital, making himself a total aggravation, one near to fanaticism, in the pursuit of the impossible, cost be damned. The tender, methodical man who had, decades earlier, faced suffering and extinction in the tangled jungles of an Asian peninsula with stoicism, could not begin to handle the deterioration that, inexorably, consumed the life of his wife.

His degree of unacceptance was far beyond the norms of grief. Andy and Meg, the resilience of youth their greatest ally, helped their father in a role reversal of counsel. Without them, he would certainly have, one way or another, followed Cassandra to the cemetery, where twin plots were green and manicured.

At St. Luke's the ceremony was conducted before a modest group of friends. There were no relatives within a thousand miles and distant cousins had been long neglected by both sides. Neighbors, women friends, a few employees from Cardinal Hardware and, in a rear pew, silent and withdrawn, Zack Taylor and his family and Tom DeShales, came to pay last respects to a woman he had never met. Andy spoke briefly in reminiscence of his mother, his voice strong and emotional, never faltering. Meg tried her best to follow him, but after a few struggling words, could not continue. Zack Taylor considered adding to the eulogy, in fact started to make a move, reconsidered and remained in his seat. I might break down like Meg, he thought, and that would be a botched tribute to the memory of his friend.

After the funeral cortege to the resting place, Galen, at home with friends and children seemed, almost miraculously, to rebound, his spirit reaching, at last, a plateau of acceptance. The past two summers of my life, he thought, have nearly finished me. But, for her sake, I should carry on and show some semblance of guidance for Andy and Meg, all that remains of the Janes family. I wrestled unendingly with my wife's adventures a year ago, my ambivalence drained me. This summer I watched, with helplessness, the fading of that buoyant, irreverent life force, a force I never really understood, but could only love. We were in many ways an unmatched pair. I, with my plodding, plebian ways and Cassandra, the ultimate independent, thumbing her nose at convention and daring the establishment to take her down.

Cassandra, with no special training or talent beyond raw guts, whipped the world. Then she encountered, as all of us eventually must, an enemy that would not bargain with her and could not be overcome by wit or daring.

Like the pirates of old, Cassandra, a modern buccaneer, sailed under no man's flag but her own. She raided with abandon, she went out with dignity, never complaining, never surrendering, a class act until the final curtain. The woman had an unclear vision, strange, clouded perhaps, but she followed her stars until the stars faded away in the cruel light of day.

The Criminal Housewife

CHAPTER 25

The duck blind was a good one, if there is any such thing. The reeds were thick and tall and the flat bottomed boat provided an adequate stand for the hunters, their shotguns, the dog, and the odd decoys now already bobbing in the slow current of the Mississippi backwater. But, as any non-hunter would aver, the early morning atmosphere was gray, dismal, wet and windy. Duck hunters, like deer and antelope hunters are a breed apart; they relish their misery, warm comfort is for the faint of heart, and call it euphoric.

And a slice of heaven it was for Zack Taylor and Tom DeShales. Two birds had been bagged, one by each, and the dog, belonging to Zack, had paddled out and blissfully retrieved them. The two men hoped for more harvest before returning to Crestburg and another working day.

"I must be out of my mind," groaned DeShales. "Out of the sack at three-thirty, bolt down iodine coffee and black toast, no butter, damn the diet, to get my ass forty miles down here to freeze."

"You love it."

"I know I do. That's what frightens me. I fear for my sanity."

"A little late. Hey, quick!" Zack raised his gun and fired a fast two shells from his over and under. Destroyer, the bird dog, splashed into the water and brought back the sodden prize. "I ought to be a trick shot artist in the circus. I'm that good."

"Lucky shot."

"My luck does seem to persist."

More ducks appeared but at a distance, the decoys disdained. Shots were fired but to no result. Destroyer sulked beside them.

DeShales asked, with true concern, "Are you getting over it?"

"Oh, sure. We live, we die, takes in everybody one time or another."

"Oh, man, just shouldn't be. Forty-six years old, wasn't she?"

"Just turned. Less than two months ago."

"Roll of the dice."

"Funny you said that. Cassandra often used that expression. Kind of a sign of her fatalism."

"See her often, last couple months?"

"Yeah, I did. Quite a bit. She needed me for some legal stuff. Draw up her will, make some other arrangements."

"Death watch for you, buddy."

Zack Taylor was quiet, the conversation beginning to bother him. He knew DeShales meant well, was, in fact, quite sympathetic. But he drew back from displays of emotion and knew he was close to the edge. How could he disclose to his friend the depth of feeling he had developed toward his favorite client? Money aside, and her cases had added greatly to his strained financial well being, he simply had grown fond of the free-wheeling blonde, the true, blue lady, as he had come to think of her.

"You're right, Tom. Death takes no holiday." Zack sighed. "She had the best of care, the Clinic pulled out all the stops for Cassandra. But some cancers metastasize like wild fire. Some day, someday, who knows?" His voice trailed off, despondency upon him.

DeShales sensed the mood.

"I grieve for you, Zack. The loss of a wonderful friend. And what unbelievable turns and twists in the road."

"For sure."

"Mrs. Janes - Cassandra - gets involved, by the long arm of coincidence, in a couple of law suits, potential suits anyway, is awarded compensations for her character assassination and, later, her injuries. She and hubby take a long trip abroad and the curtain descends."

"The long arm of fate. Sweeps wider than any of us can know."

"And sweeps the just and the unjust alike. And who among us can judge which is which?"

"We've got learned judges on the bench that struggle with such matters." Zack was pensive in the gray morning. "I only hope to God, if I'm not being a bit presumptuous, that she had a wonderful time on the trip although, I assume, for Galen's sake, she faked it a bit toward the end as her discomfort increased. She would, you know."

"Fake things?"

"Well, don't we all one time or another? Do you ever fake great interest in real estate deals that bore you to tears?"

"Don't even ask. Meets and Bounds, lot lines, drainage ditches, ponds, cul-de-sacs." DeShales, cold and damp, was in his complaining mood. "Surveys, assessments, annexations – what a mountain of paper. And if one, just one, regulation is screwed up or missed, the government pounces, like a bobcat on a bunny."

"Is there a rest home for real estate attorneys?"

"There should be. And if they have old ladies there, like Shirl, they'll be babbling in their soup."

"Trouble again?"

"Not yet, but looming. I've been toeing the line like a Boy Scout. But it's never enough. Drill sergeants could take lessons from that red head."

"Aw, well, don't borrow trouble. You still have a sweet body to warm your bed. And so do I, for that matter."

The euphoria of the morning had worn thin as the time moved past seven-thirty. "Three birds, not much of a haul," averred DeShales. "But let's call it a morning, get back to town. I'll see you for a drink at five. OK?"

"Done."

The two attorneys drove back to town, the autumn scenery as beautiful in its way as the verdant colors of spring and summer. Now the dominant hues were gold, in both bright and subdued tones. This was corn and soybean country. Both crops were in various stages of harvest, some still in the field, others already harvested with the soil showing dark from fall plowing. The same old story held true each year, farmers hurrying to beat the coming snow with early picking, city folks hoping the harvest was delayed for better hunting. Tom and Zack had their occasional fling at pheasant hunting but preferred the marshy challenge of waterfowl, wet and bone chilling though it usually was.

In the late afternoon they met again in the funky half-light of the East Side Bar, an ancient establishment without a liquor license, beer only, but lots of it, and reasonable. Cigarette smoke, blue and heavy, hung near the low ceiling. Emphysema ward was one of the kindest local terms but the neighborly ambience was a welcome change from the tonier bistros of downtown.

"So," said DeShales, "here we have a family, remnants of a family, at least, always poor, forever scrambling and, lately, wealthy. And the lady who made it all possible, gone."

"But not forgotten."

"Understood. But how is the fortune divided? Just a transfer to Galen, I imagine."

"Not exactly."

"Hm – what then?"

"I'm not at liberty to say. The probate hearing is next week. I'm executor."

"That I did not know."

"Well, when all the events of last year were going on, I sort of became, by default, the family solicitor." Now Zack Taylor was serious, professional. "Ethically, I'm sealed until we've met with family and probate judge."

"Of course, I wasn't prying. Even if it is my perverted nature to be nosy."

"Aw, no offense, Tom." Zack grasped his friend's shoulder. "It's just that I was the man who drew up the will to Cassandra's exact specs. Almost too late. Cassandra was fading fast. A week later we could not have communicated."

"All this at the hospital?"

"Of course. And I don't mind admitting to you, my friend, that the whole business tore me apart. I had a hard time. Cassandra, on the way out, was magnificent. She was actually comforting me. Yeah, me, the tough guy."

"So you're wrapped up in the whole scene. Taxes, certificates, funeral home, cemetery, all claims, if any. All that stuff."

"You named it, all that stuff, the legalese that lubricates our system for both the living and the dead."

"Has to be."

"I know – I know. And the fee is quite generous. Just wish it wasn't me."

DeShales ordered a refill. Tap beer. What bottled brew could compare?

"Cassandra can rest easy that her worldly affairs are in your hands. I mean that."

"Thanks."

"The good die young. Isn't that what they say?"

"Oh, hell, they say a lot of things. The good, the bad and the ugly, remember Clint Eastwood? They die when their time comes." Zack, restless, drank deeply, savoring the collar. "I gotta get off this. I'll be getting maudlin."

"Just an old softy."

"I suppose. But that isn't all bad, the older I get, the more I'm convinced that sentiment, instead of being ridiculed, should be praised. Too much harshness, an overabundance of cynicism in the world."

"I left my violin at home," scoffed DeShales. "You're

one of the toughest sons of bitches I know. I'd just as soon tangle with a gator as you. You can be mean as sin and you did win a case for a hard boiled lady, no matter how nice. Now come Mr. goody buns."

Zack Taylor took the lecture calmly. "You're right, of course, I tend to get a little preachy. You and I are in a confrontational line of work. Not physical, like pro wrestling but, sometimes, just as contrived." He finished his brew. "I'm looking for a balance, Tom. Hard, tough, but fair – and with an appreciation of the other guy's point of view."

"Believe it or not, I strive for the same. Trying to be like a rock, but not vindictive. Applies to personal matters, too. Take Shirl."

"I pass."

"Making my point, barrister. Shirl has treated me like dirt. I have a hell of a time seeing things from her viewpoint but, now and again, I stop and think what if I was a good looking, free wheeling, unfettered gal like Shirl,.,~

"Long stretch for me."

"I know, this is just supposing. Let me elaborate on this thesis. I'd hate to be tied to a fatuous, grumpy, self-centered ass hole like me. I'd get restless, I'd be inclined to get the hell out, like rats deserting a sinking ship."

"Well, yeah, you put it like that."

"This," said DeShales, "is a watermark in our relationship, acquaintanceship, whatever tag you put on this sorry Abbot and Costello act. The man hardly ever agrees with me, except when I put myself down. Then, yeah, Tom, you're dead right."

"I call 'em as I see 'em."

DeShales laughed and finished his beer. A change of pace. "OK for poker, Friday?"

"Absolutely. The planets are in orbit. Or not. The earth revolves smoothly. Or wobbles. But a good game of poker is better than a good piece – of apple pie."

"You're a smooth talker, Zack. Don't stutter like that."

DeShales was morose. "Apple pie has been hard to find lately at our house."

"You going to catch something sweet, you gotta bait the trap."

"Last winter, if you recall, I plunged for a new BMW. If that ain't baiting the damn trap, what the hell is? Do I have to go the mink coat route?"

"Tom – Tom. Do I gotta draw you a picture? You're talking things, just material things. What I meant was sweetheart stuff, the nice words, the caresses, all that Cosmopolitan Magazine female jargon."

"Yeah, I know. Doesn't come as easy to me as a smooth drummer like you."

"Drummer?"

"Old time word for salesman. Read it in a book some damn place."

The Criminal Housewife

CHAPTER 26

One month had passed since the last defenseless ducks had been blasted out of the sky. Some animal rights wags have suggested that it is not really a sport, that to qualify as such, the ducks should be given the opportunity to shoot back. "I've heard of that theory," said Zack Taylor. "Actually has certain egalitarian aspects, but, hell, just not practical. I mean, where would they get the weapons? How would they aim and fire, not being equipped with the endowment of a trigger finger?"

"I've considered those matters, myself," said Tom DeShales. "Really, the problems seem insurmountable. And they would have to lay for us among the rushes, pull a surprise raid. It's tough to shoot from the wing, so to speak. As talented as I am with the over and under, I don't believe I could manage."

"There is another aspect to the fairness question," averred Zack. "The birds do have weapons. We have occasionally been splattered and we have been unable to respond in kind."

So went learned discussion in the weathered duck boat in the backwaters of the big Miss, the mighty river that splits a continent and defines east and west. There was no ranting this time on the capriciousness of the weatherman. In early dawn the temperature hovered around fifty-four, with warm sunshine promised for a gorgeous fall day.

"So what's with Madge?" An innocent question,

directed to DeShales.

"What the hell do you know about Madge? I mean – what do you mean?"

"Come on, Tom. I could count on my toes the people in Crestburg who are unaware that your lovely secretary has adored you for years. She doesn't really hide it, you know."

"Madge is a very competent woman. We get along fine. And the rest of the world can mind their own business."

"Agreed. But you know the world. They don't usually go along with live and let live."

"Then why the subject?"

"Because Tom, we're friends. For a long time and I hope, forever. I know you and Shirl are in enemy camps again. Hell, you got to be somewhere, pal, and I feel for what you're up against."

DeShales wiped his face with a handkerchief. He was clearly shaken. "It's been hell, Zack. After twenty-two years, good and bad, the trouble is off the charts. Sure, I've had Madge out for lunch a few times. She deserves it."

"Deserves lunch for sure. Maybe more."

The subject was closed. Ducks were tardy in making an appearance. "We should have sprung for new decoys this year," muttered Zack. "The word's gotten out among the feathered brethren. 'These ain't ducks fellows. They're wooden imitations by a lousy artist.'"

"One of those birds is a lawyer, I swear. Handing out legal advice and precautions to the flock."

"Gets paid in extra corn, gleaned from all the bumper crops this year."

A tiny flock of ducks appeared to the east, veering slightly as though intrigued by the wooden simulations. As they neared, both men fired and, amazingly, two birds plummeted into the river. Destroyer, frantic for action, fetched them in.

"In the estate of your finest and most productive client, what happened, Zack?"

Zack Taylor sighed. He knew he had to level with DeShales, had promised as much, and this was as good a time as any. They were bobbing in a backwater, far from any prying eyes or ears. So he recalled the details, long friendship would seal the secrecy.

"Everything went as Cassandra had devised, not to the penny, of course. While she was still with us, there were tag ends on her investments and accounts. But percentage-wise, we got the job done. She should rest easy."

"The lot to the family, I assume."

"You are so wrong. But, understandably, I would have predicted the same." Zack Taylor had mourned and wept at the death of his favorite client. He found talking about the fact almost unbearable. "She lumped off the complete stash, subtracted taxes, funeral costs, honorarium to the minister, the soloist, all that traditional stuff that follows most folks to the grave. Then, twenty-five thousand off the top for my boy, Billy. Can you believe it? She'd never met the lad, but studied the syndrome while in the hospital.

"That is magnificent."

"I know. Anyway, when everything had been accounted for, as best as we could predict, there remained two million, three hundred thousand and some odd dollars."

"Sizeable."

"Yes. And that is where the percentages entered the picture. Straight down the middle, one half to her family, one half to charity. Or, in Cassandra's own words, one half to the world and the people who need it the most."

"You're not putting me on?" DeShales incredulity was apparent.

"I would never do that. Check that statement. I <u>would</u> put you on. But not on something like this."

"How does it break down?"

"First of all, in a gesture to the youthful activities of Meg, one hundred thousand dollars to Habitat for

Humanity."

"I don't know much about them."

"It's the outfit that Jimmy Carter works for in his busy retirement. I think the ex prez has gone to Haiti, places like that, to help with structures for the desolate and homeless. But mostly they're for the U.S. of A. lower class. I hate that designation 'lower class' - much too elitist for my taste, but you know what I mean."

"Yeah. Who is upper class? People with a lot of bucks, I presume."

"We can't get into that right now," sighed Zack. "But Habitat doesn't sugar coat their good deeds. They require participation, sweat equity from the fortunate recipients. Also, they rely heavily on volunteer contributions of labor and material from building craftsmen and contractors. Hell of a system."

"Then, after the one hundred grand to the house builders, you've got over a million dollars remaining."

"Cassandra said she had a lot of pet projects, like her old church, St. Luke's, the library, fire and police, and so on." 'I'm too bushed, Zack, to sort it all out,' she said. 'Just take the lot and give it to the Community Chest or United Way, as they now call it. They'll work it out to the best advantage of the town.' Those aren't her exact words, but damn close. So we drew it up that way."

"Amazing."

"Not all that uncommon, Tom. Some folks on the way out feel this tremendous debt of gratitude to the city that has been their earthly abode. The money came, one way or another, from society. Give it back to society in a fashion to help the most needy people." Zack paused for a long moment. "I'm not giving you my views, you understand. But Cassandra had a fierce allegiance to the less fortunate. 'I got lucky,' she said, 'other people, most of them better and smarter than me, don't hit the jackpot. Maybe this begins to even the score.'"

"There is one hell of a lot of wisdom in that. The other half go to Galen?"

"Yes and no. To the family. One half of the undedicated goes to Galen, one quarter each to Andy and Meg. She said to me, 'that stubborn husband of mine is skittish on this money, says it wasn't earned. But I think he'll take that much. What he does with it is his business. Hope he gets a new wardrobe and, damnit, a new wife. He's such a darling, caring man. I just want him to be happy and well provided for. The quarter million plus for both Andy and Meg will get them a start in life, the opportunity they need, with no chance of becoming rich, spoiled brats. Oh, hell, they wouldn't anyway, but too much easy money tends to corrode the soul.' For a hustling gal, Cass had a lot of human wisdom."

"After all this, I can't believe you think of her as a hustler."

"I don't. Not in the accepted sense of the word. But she sure wanted money for herself and the family. When Boles apologized for the false detention, she could well have said OK, forget it, and gone on her way. She didn't. When she suffered the busted arm and other diverse injuries in Minneapolis, she could certainly have accepted medical treatment, which, incidentally, was a tacit admission of negligence by the airport people. But no, she hustled, with my guidance, the big settlements in each case. That's all I mean."

"Isn't it strange, Zack? Cassandra, I mean. I never met the lady. Still it seems she has been a part of my life. I could almost see her, from your descriptions and I was deeply impressed."

"We come in contact with a few people in our lives that are that unforgettable. Whatever she was, whatever angels or demons drove that feisty spirit, she was so damn likeable."

"I'll never meet anyone in my line of work that will work that magic. Not in the real estate game, not in a thousand years." DeShales mourned the dullness of his life.

"You complaining again, or yet?"

"Yeah, guess so."

"Well," said Zack Taylor, "I've put it all behind me now. Other battles to fight, other fish to fry. You know how it goes."

"Sure. And other ducks to clean and dress, messy as the job may be."

Zack scoffed. "You one of those Park Avenue sportsmen? Love to shoot, the thrill of the hunt, the danger, the excitement?"

"What danger?"

"The boat might swamp. The dog might bite you, stuff like that. Or I might level at a low flying bird and shoot you instead."

"I have thought of that," admitted DeShales.

"Anyway, a true sportsman follows through. I know some guys expect their wives to clean and dress the game their husbands, the noble hunters and gatherers bring back to the cave."

"If I laid one of these muddy specimens in front of Shirl, then I'd learn what real danger is. Shirl thinks – oh, hell, she thinks a lot of strange things." DeShales was despondent.

"You're a slow student, Tom. I've taught you all I know about hunting and fishing and you still know zilch. I can't help you on the personal stuff."

They drove back to the city, Zack Taylor to the home of an injured client, DeShales back to his office. A mountain of work awaited him, he should never have borrowed the time for mallards. He worked at a killing pace for two hours, seeking to relax in work, but his mind was in turmoil. DeShales knew the changes in his life status were closing in, that decisions long postponed must be faced. Ambivalent, as always, he both anticipated and dreaded what lay ahead.

Madge Evans worked alongside him. She had a keen paralegal mind and had, through the years, saved DeShales from scores of mistakes. More than a secretary, she was, except in title, a member of the firm. A bear for work, she was always reliable, while her boss had streaks of productivity and periods of carelessness. Whatever I botch up, he thought, Madge will catch the errors. This was his operating theory and he knew the woman had virtually adopted him and lived her life in jealousy of Shirl.

He wearied. "Where shall we go for lunch today? I'm famished after a morning in the boonies."

"I'd rather order in, Tom."

"OK. Any special reason?"

"You know there's a reason, darling. People." She blushed, but was firm.

"Sure, I know. People. I could say hell with 'em but that's no good. We have to change the situation."

"What do you mean?"

"We work in a world of legality." He put his arms around her and held her close. "And legal it shall be before many months have passed if I'm not mistaken."

"You're singing my song."

"I don't like to sing a song of procrastination, honey. Must seem to you like a stall sometimes."

"Oh, hell, I know what you're up against, Tom. She'll have the paint off your car if she has a chance. Or the laces right out of your shoes."

"You're tough, darling, But you're right."

The Criminal Housewife

CHAPTER 27

The long cold arm of another Minnesota winter had swept through the months to March. A mild winter, with below average snowfall, had modified the usual winter blues and softened cabin fever to a tolerable level.

A measure of normalcy returned to Galen Janes. Neither his ordinary life nor his long travail in Vietnam had prepared this gentle man for the devastation of his bereavement. But grief is conquered, losses are put behind. Galen, always the involved parent, provided whatever homespun guidance he could manage.

Meg, in her brand new Honda, was pretty, popular and apparently very little impressed with herself or her finances. She dated a boisterous, amusing high school senior who was often left stranded on weekends while the devoted young woman served as helper and gofer for her favorite organization. Habitat for Humanity had held a brief ceremony for the memory of Cassandra Janes and her gift. Meg was determined to give life and sweat equity to the challenge of helping the dispossessed find a measure of hope and comfort.

Andy kept his minimum hours, often only seven or eight a week, at Acme. He felt a need, an urgency to keep contact with the industrial world and the banter and friendship of the workers added a comfortable balance to his life. His academic career soared and he was well placed, poised for his future entrance into the wonders and brutal study of law.

With both of her children, Cassandra, the supreme

scam artist, had gambled well. Both knew the quiet confidence of a quarter million in reserve. Both had been, out of necessity, well immersed in the family tradition that money was not to be frivolously wasted but guarded for lifetime needs and emergencies.

Meg was at home with Galen. She was actually a better housekeeper and cook than her mother, who had handled such obligations with a cavalier attitude that all this fuss was not really necessary. The girl worried about her Dad, urged him toward new horizons, to meet new people. Like a prom hostess with a bashful sophomore, she knew, instinctively, that mingling was a needed therapy. Galen had more than enough leisure. He, too, had cut back on work against the mild protestations of the Cardinal boss. He was now working twenty hours a week. "You can't spend all that precious time in your basement shop, Dad," Meg insisted. "Not when there are scads of nice women out there who are also lonely."

Galen grinned at this and began, cautiously, the initial stages of something resembling a social life. He was resigned and, in a way, gratified for his financial freedom but, like Andy and Meg, not overwhelmed. None of his limited circle of friends had any idea of the half million plus in his account. As he had told Cassandra, he would never leave the old story-and-a-half on the tree lined avenue that had been his home since Nam. The money is there, he thought, and though I didn't earn it, I won't turn into a crabby miser, but the money will be tended and grown. Like a garden.

The driven man searched for balance in his existence in a part of the country where he had once found renewed friendship with an old army buddy, Nick Evans, in the untamed mountain area of eastern Tennessee. Nick had aided Galen in a remarkable assignment when money was needed to release Andy from his youthful drug debts. The first visit of the veterans had been a roaring drunken success and old bonds had been reforged.

Looking back, Galen marveled at what they had accomplished together. "Aw hell, it wasn't much, Gale," offered Nick. "A little risky, sure, but not like hauling moonshine. Now <u>that</u> is a hairy proposition. The pay is good if you live to collect and your rig doesn't get shot up or blown away. Folks around here are mighty touchy about territory and who horns in on the other guy."

Galen laughed at all this, his first light heartedness in many months. He understood little of his old friend's acceptance of living on the edge. But the mountain air, the fishing and companionship nursed his spirit back toward normalcy. One element was missing from the scene. Nick's sister, a free spirit who had adored Galen, as did her two boys, had remarried and moved to other mountains, other streams in Idaho. Galen took this news with quiet acceptance. Samantha loved me once, he though. I had a little spunk then, now I'm middle-aged, next thing to an old man, the monotony of every day life at the store, and my loss have broken me down. Samantha's well off without me.

Galen enjoyed his time with the rugged old ex-sergeant but after ten days, he was ready to leave. The old story, he thought, things are never the same the second time. The old house, without a woman's touch, was rundown, unkempt. Weeds clogged the yard and the flower bed was gone. Even the hound dog had died and had not been replaced.

The visit had been a disappointment, an attempt, almost desperately, to recapture a past that was gone forever. There is no peace for me in this lovely corner of the earth, he thought. The preachers tell us that true peace comes only from within and they may well be right. Time heals. I've been too impatient. One factor comforted him; no one had been injured in Cassandra's forays except the woman herself.

Galen recalled, with a smile, asking Cassandra at the beginning if she planned to use a gun. The question had not been frivolous, visions of Bonnie and Clyde had surfaced. Bank robberies, ala the Liberation Army of Patty Hearst, employee thefts, cooking the books, drug smuggling, selling phantom merchandise from a P.O. address – how many ways have humans invented to separate people from their money? Many are fraught with violence, many merely devious. Cassandra, in her voracious appetite, had taken the road of non-violence, a criminal who wouldn't harm a mouse.

Back in Crestburg he pondered, endlessly, the dichotomy of his new found affluence. What are the implications of my involvement? Where does all this stack up in the cosmic picture or is it so insignificant that it's little more than a blip on the big screen, a landscape that's strewn with the fallout of corporate scams so immense as to be beyond law or regulation? And what are the cleansing properties of a million plus directed in an astounding will to the benefit of others, most of them people that Cassandra could have never known. Does one hand wash the other? The dilemma is, my position on the inheritance is that it's not rightly mine and yet I cannot dishonor the last wish of my wife, a woman who was the light of my life and one who never ceased to care. I'm happy that the few people involved at United Way are sworn to secrecy on the identity of the anonymous donor. That wish has also been fulfilled.

***

Zack Taylor's practice was flourishing. Tired of exclusive injury litigation, he expanded gradually into family law. He passed up a number of lucrative divorce cases, urging reconciliation when possible. Billy remained at home. Professionals continually urged institutionalizing the silent boy, but the Taylors would have no part of it. They hoped that Billy was happy with home care and felt he would feel betrayed if sent away and whatever chances there were for improvement

206

would be forever lost. On this, logic and statistics were against them, but where was there a measurement for love? Zack and his wife knew of no such balance.

Zack Taylor's old fishing and hunting buddy was now a newlywed. He and Shirl had, with surprisingly little rancor, divorced and now she occupied the big house on the hill. On the unfair settlement, Tom DeShales shed no tears; he considered the arrangement a bargain. The rotund lawyer and Madge has wasted little time in tying the knot and moving into a handsome condo near the center of town.

In the expanding mood of the city, burgeoning with new homes and businesses, the realm of real estate legal opportunities kept him busy. Not too involved to give up the poker games and the search for walleyes and mallards. but still heavily booked. What Zack had commented on was true. His secretary had adored him for years and, effortlessly, moved in to fill the empty void, guiding her man with a loose rein.

Shirl had for her part actually put some effort into a good relationship with her husband. A second honeymoon had followed his spying expedition and carried them for many months. But, as DeShales suspected, the taste of diesel fuel was in her blood, now she was involved with a rugged truck driver and spent many days and nights with him on the long hauls. Tom DeShales' sorry attempt at sleuthing at the Oil Derrick had produced no telling evidence but he had been as much unlucky as inept. For often, in the history of the stormy marriage, Shirl had found solace and comfort and a wild surge of adventure in the padded sleeping space behind the cab of more than one King of the Road.

End